# HALF BREED

*Finding Unity in a Divided World*

ISBN: 978-1-949709-57-5
Cover design by: Printopya
Photo by: Meshali Mitchell
For Worldwide Distribution, Printed in the USA.

# TABLE OF CONTENTS

# FOREWORD

I am so honored to write this foreword for my friend LeTesha Wheeler. While writing I thought of how forewords in books are sometimes overlooked, just like many of the signs giving us a forward direction in life. Sometimes, it's hard to see a sign in front of you, but once you see it, it's hard to unsee it. For example, you're probably familiar with the logo for FedEx. Staring at it, it appears as a regular logo, but have you ever noticed the arrow that is pointing forward within the logo? It's not easy to notice at first, but once you see it, it's hard to unsee it. Every time I see a FedEx truck, I look at the logo and notice the sign of the forward arrow within it. Now, I cannot *not* see it. In other words, it is hard to unsee. Signs in life are like that as well, aren't they? We take them for granted at first, but before long, we see another facet that we can't unsee, and we are faced with choosing to move forward in the direction of the sign.

One of the greatest signs God used in the Bible to point the way forward was families. Some families became living signs and wonders to Israel. Isaiah the prophet's family was one of them, and he mentions this in Isaiah 8:18, which says, "I and the children whom the Lord has given me, are for signs and wonders in Israel . . ." Isaiah wasn't merely talking about how his family walked in signs and wonders, but he was saying his entire family is a sign and a wonder for the nation. Their family became the prophetic statement and their lives spoke louder than words. They confirmed God's will and confronted all opposition through the prophetic statement, which was their life. This is true not only for Isaiah and his family but for you and me as well. When a man and a woman come together in holy matrimony, that marriage becomes a sign of loving possibilities.

This especially is the case when it comes to interracial marriages. Everyone wonders, "What brought that black man to the white woman? [or vice versa] How did they meet? Don't they know that's not what we expect around here?" All the while, as people wonder at the love of the opposite hues, the fruit of their union becomes signs. Their children become signs of the love they share, all wrapped in human flesh.

In Isaiah 62, where God is speaking of His desire for Jerusalem, He says that Jerusalem will no longer be called forsaken but rather "My delight is in her" and that "her land shall be called married." In Jewish custom, the marriage of the land was one of the greatest aspects of the union of the husband and wife. Lands were combined naturally and became one, resulting also in the spiritual healing of the land. Spiritually, all of humanity is composed of the land of the earth, because we are descendants of Adam, who was made of land: the dust of the earth. And every time a marriage covenant happens and people unite, more land gets married, united and healed. And the fruit of that united land bears the expression of love, in the manifestation of what we call today mixed-race children. Through the minds and eyes of many, when people of polar extremes of race and ethnic hues marry, the fruit of their union creates the most recognizably and undeniably beautiful babies on the planet. They represent the beauty of land being healed by love.

Even the most hardened hearts cannot deny the beauty of "mixed-race" or "half-breed" babies. Whether black or white, brown, yellow, or red, there is no denying how children of these united lands are beautiful. But are they really that much more beautiful, or are we more aware of a new possibility of love that was previously unseen? The reality is that because crossing color and ethnic lines are still somewhat taboo, their striking features jars us all into a possibility beyond bias, and the children become a prophetic statement to the power of love. They represent the beauty of land being healed by love. As a result, we are introduced to another facet of the *imago dei*: children born in a beautiful image of God. Their beauty was unrealized before we saw them, because of our own shallowness due to barriers. And once they are seen, that beautiful expression is hard to unsee. And what is powerful is when we get to see and hear their expression and understanding of the world, and how to heal the division within it. Unfortunately, that love has been fraught with resistance for years.

Just as people abused Christianity to oppress during slavery, religious and misguided people blinded by racism and ignorance have used the Bible to keep different ethnicities from marrying. From Bible teachers like Finis Jennings Dakes, who taught that race mixing was against the will of God, to laws that prevented people of different races to marry, the resistance of man against change and interracial marriage continued for years. Yet all that shifted through the power of a loving relationship, which became a sign, through the courtship and marriage of the Lovings.

In 1958 in the state of Virginia, interracial marriage was illegal and punishable with jail time. This law wasn't only in Virginia but also in 24 states. The case of Richard and Mildred Loving's lawsuit was appealed all the way to the Supreme Court. Finally, love eventually was supreme to hate and division, as the court sided with the Lovings in 1967. With the barriers down, more interracial couples took courage and married all over the country. Since then, a "Loving Generation" has been born, who are the children of those interracial unions, who have given us their powerful stories. From their stories we learn from their unique lives with their distinct inherited opportunities and demands. For example:

> They learn two different ways of seeing life through the lens of color from their parents.
> They grow up eating two different ethnic cuisines on holidays, learn two different languages, dialects and slang.
> They grow up learning to understand both sides of an argument and perspectives before they offer their opinion.

Their search for identity and meaning is unique, and once in Christ, they offer to us a perspective of seeing the love of God through their understanding. I believe God is using the offspring of interracial united love to heal our land. Their biblical worldview and perspective are hard to unsee, once they are explained. And you need to learn from their perspective, because there's probably more to your own background than you realize. You will learn if you search far enough in your own genealogy that we are all "mixed-race," all "half breeds" of some type, as members of the only true race, the human race. Yet, how does the Gospel address our identity issues? What is God's remedy for healing our hurt from division? What is the way forward for America or other nations dealing with racial tensions or ethnic strife? These questions and more are addressed and answered in this book by its amazing author.

LeTesha Wheeler, a beautiful byproduct of an interracial marriage, has now emerged as a voice from the Loving Generation. And I believe God has raised her up as a sign with a message that can heal our land. My friend has put together one of the best biblical understandings of social justice and of healing the racial divide that I've read. She poignantly discusses issues of race and discrimination in the Bible with great doctrinal insight. I highly recommend this book because it addresses identity issues and the power of the Gospel to heal every racial and class division. In this book, she is honest and transparent and helps you understand her American experience and all the beauty associated with being the child of courageous parents who decided to love beyond society's boundaries. LeTesha is a loving sign, pointing the way forward to what God is doing to heal America. This is a powerful book filled with hope for our nations. After you read this book, it will be hard to unsee God's handiwork in your life.

Will Ford III

Chair, Marketplace Leadership, Christ For The Nations Institute, Dallas, TX

Co-author of *The Dream King: How the Dream of Martin Luther King Jr. Is Being Fulfilled to Heal Racism in America*

Founder, Dream Stream Company (www.dreamstreamco.com)

Founder, 818 The Sign (www.818thesign.org)

Email: will@818thesign.org

# PREFACE

The word "reconcile" is defined as restoring friendship or harmony. In essence, racial reconciliation is to restore or harmonize broken walls between races. In 2017, I heard a message on the topic of racial reconciliation, where the speaker shared details of the Samaritan half breed who overcame racial prejudice to serve another. This message came shortly after the controversy in the NFL over standing versus kneeling for the national anthem that had sparked conversations in the workplace, at home, and inundated social media nationwide.

My pastor, Mike Hayes, has pursued great work on racial reconciliation for the last thirty years in Dallas. As a Caucasian male, he has helped those who are privileged to understand that, while they may not have contributed personally to racism, it is not enough to stop there. He teaches that privilege must take it a step further to intentionally reconcile division.

I spoke with him in November 2017, after I found myself uncharacteristically stirred by the racial tension and conversations in our country, as if I were called to join in this massive task of unifying the divided nation. I asked him what he thought the answer was for the *other side*, the ones who have been hurt, oppressed, and offended by injustice for years and generations. He has been a pastor for forty years and one who has walked in unifying races for decades. I was looking for a quick answer to share with others, but he encouraged me to ask God for myself.

I did not like that answer. I felt that he was way more qualified to answer that question than I was. Plus, it would have been easier for me to just quote him instead of deriving my own opinion. But I am thankful, because what he understood is that we all have our very own specific assignments to carry out here on this earth, that come with very specific individual instructions. He has his and I have mine.

After pouting for a few minutes, I decided I would pray about it. By January 2018, I got the answer on my birthday. My dear friend Norene gave me a memorable birthday gift. She shared the Bible passage of the good Samaritan. She stated she felt my friendship with her reflected the story of the good Samaritan, living a life of serving others in love and compassion. While I thought she was being extremely generous, it also ignited something deep inside of me.

I discovered a very specific strategy within the story that was eye-opening. To walk in complete unity, we must intentionally go out of our way to love and serve others despite our own pains, obstacles, or injustices we have experienced. After doing some research I realized I relate to the Samaritan half breed not just in theory but because I, too, have mixed blood. My mother is Caucasian. My father is African American. The Samaritan is mixed Jew and Assyrian. We both are half breeds.

By the end of January, I could see that something must be done. My life experiences as a half breed, along with my faith, allowed me to develop an ability to love, serve, and give to others who are hurting, bringing reconciliation into their lives. I am the person I am today—a reconciler—because of Jesus and what He has done for me. My faith in Him has provided me with healing and the ability to walk in wholeness despite any brokenness I experienced from being *half* anything.

This topic, however, terrified me, and I was worried about the repercussions of facing this head-on through my writing. That said, I knew that I must obey and trust God more than I feared man. I finally shared with my husband, James, who is my confidant, about my daring courage to write this book though I was not sure what form it would take. To my joy, he immediately cheered on the mission. I actually tried to write a fictional short story that paralleled the parable; however, James, who is extremely honest, told me I was not on the right track. I was mad at him for telling me that but am so thankful now for his honesty that always keeps me on track.

The journey has had its own battles. I was told by top literary agents that, while this is a topic that we need to address and discuss in America, people simply want to ignore it. I was told that bookstores would potentially run from the title because of the sensitive nature of today's climate. While at times that was discouraging, it reminded me even more that this was an assignment given to me, designed for me, literally down to my DNA. In the DC Comics movie *Aquaman*, the story's hero says that he was born from two different worlds—ocean and land—in order to bring them together. I believe that is also my mission—to be a bridge builder.

This book is for anyone looking to bridge the gaps within the racial divide. I want to invite and welcome any person, of any faith, of any walk of life to join me in finding a solution for peace, unity, and justice for all in our country. I am a person of faith and sought the Bible for answers. Even if you are not a follower of the faith of Christianity, you will enjoy the content. I will refer to some biblical references, stories and Scriptures to walk out my points, but it will be easy for anyone to follow. Bear with me even if you do not agree, believe, or support this particular faith; you will likely agree with the moral and ethical guidelines discussed.

We all have a choice in how we respond to injustice. I choose to seek God's heart on the matter. I did not have an answer to division or discrimination until I started searching for a resolution. This book is the result of what I found on my journey. This is what I found: the broken, the divided, the oppressed, and the discriminated all have the secret to unlock healing and reconciliation. It is what Jesus displayed for us while He walked here on Earth and what has been recorded in the gospels as an example for us to follow. God established social justice. It was not established by activists or a certain political party. It was God's idea, and He demonstrated it through Jesus.

The Bible is used as a historical reference around the globe as it is the oldest book in history and correlates with people, places, and events from world historians. If you will join me in accessing these Bible references for the historical or morally good content, I believe this book will have great impact in your life. Chapter 11 is more of a "state of the union" address to those of the faith as it challenges the Church to stand in true love and righteousness. All are invited to read chapter 11 but not required.

If you want to find unity and peace for your family, friends, and community, I hope your heart will be open and willing to accept the challenge of restoring this great country through reconciliation by setting aside your own opinions for a time in order to find solutions along with me.

I would like to thank my mom and dad, Michelle and Elward, for the life lessons; my editor, Chelsea, for helping me organize my voice; my sister Rianna and friends Amarillys, Julee Ann, Suzanne, Joel, and Michelle, for proofreading, prayers and advice; Norene, for giving me a birthday gift that would change my life forever; William and DeHavilland Ford, for giving their life to restoring our great country; Mike Hayes, for being an apostle to many nations; and last, but not least, my number-one supporter, my husband, James: I would have never been brave enough to walk this journey without you.

# INTRODUCTION

"Who is better? Black or white?" It was 1985 in Houston, Texas, and I was about four or five years old. I do not remember the specific conversation leading up to the question or what prompted this discussion, if I had said something inappropriate or if something life defining was shown on TV. Maybe we saw an interaction between neighbors. What I do know is my daddy is a good father. He was about to prepare me for a life lesson I would not forget for the next three decades. It would form the very foundation of the person I was to become—including the author of this very book.

"Tesha, who is better? Black or white?" my dad asked me.

I clearly remember my thoughts at the time—*this is an obvious answer to me*—so I answered without hesitation. "White," I said. He turned me around and spanked me.

He asked me again, "Who is better? Black or white?"

What he wanted me to say seemed even more obvious to me now, so I responded, "Black!" He turned me around and spanked me again.

He asked a third time, "Who is better? Black or white?"

"Neither," I answered.

"Correct," he said.

That memory has never left me. It gave me a deep understanding that neither was better—or worse. I was not white, and I was not black. I was both.

When I share that story, it brings me to tears. It was a life-defining moment that set the trajectory of that child forever. My father had a unique opportunity: allow me to step into bondage or encourage me to walk in freedom. His question was an invitation to break free from hatred, prejudice, or offense, and declare the freedom that Martin Luther King, Jr. and so many others marched for and that Jesus Christ ultimately died for. If I had not received the power of that message in the depths of my heart and soul that day as a child, perhaps today I would not be writing a book sharing the recipe for our nation to walk in unity, love, and compassion. The lesson I learned that day would last me a lifetime.

History books and the Bible tell us that Jews were often taken from their homes and forced to live in other countries. In ancient Israel, these displaced Jews mixed with the local people, creating a half-breed race called the Samaritans. They were outcasts, excluded from Jewish rituals and even places of worship. This practice of displacing prisoners of war and then rejecting them has been in place for thousands of years as we trace world history.

In America, there is a mixed-breed race, a race that was stolen from their land and forced to intermingle with the local foreigners but yet continued to be hated and discriminated against while trying to form an identity. We call them African Americans. Today, there are plenty of mixed races here in America, people blended from countries all over the world, which makes this nation great. Many of them came here to find life and liberty. However, we are not as united as our name would indicate. Some would say we are more divided now than during the horrific years of segregation and the height of racism in the 1950s and 1960s.

My German grandmother was an enemy of the state when she married my grandfather from New York. She fought against a system that tried to keep her behind a wall. My southern, black grandmother, Bigmama, raised a large family with my grandfather during the most segregated time in the state of Texas. She fought against a system that tried to divide the dignity of her children. My very DNA provided me the keys to unlock racial division through my personal history, culture, and journey as a half breed. This is a story of how the half breed—anyone the world tries to divide—can bring wholeness to a broken world.

I use the term "half breed" only as a description and not as an insult. The term was originally a derogatory one used to describe an individual who was both Native American and white, although now it is used to describe anyone of mixed race. It was used as an insult in films and throughout history. I did not use that term as a child, nor was I ever referred to specifically as a half breed. That said, the offensive word gives value to the issues addressed in this book, the issues our country faces today.

Most of us can likely identify with a half-breed experience. I have experienced both financial lack and abundance. I walked in faith with family roots in Baptist, Catholic, Methodist, and nondenominational churches. I am a woman of color who worked in an industry dominated by middle-aged white men, with people twice my age reporting to me. In many of these situations I felt inadequate, different, or disqualified.

In my youth, I attended thirteen different schools in three different socially, politically, and economically diverse states. By the time I reached adulthood I had gathered friends of every race, color, creed, and religion. The culturally rich and diverse life lessons I learned were the very ingredients needed to reconcile races, socioeconomic status, and gender in a divided world. My perspective was unique: I did not live a black life or a white life—it was one life:

a life that loves. Love compels us to fight against injustice. It is our responsibility.

The question we are all faced with is this: are we part of the problem or of the solution here in America? The answer is yes. It is time for us to examine our hearts, motives, and actions in order to determine how we are contributing to the problem in our country, or how we are offering a solution.

This book is broken into three phases: *The Issue, The Answer,* and *The Application.* The issues we have at hand are the problems we face today in America, including offense and ignorance. The answer challenges us with the solutions and how to address them within our hearts, homes, and community. The application demonstrates how to actually walk out the necessary healing we need in our nation in order to build bridges and bring change.

I am a practical person and I find that simple action plans are more effective, and hopeful, than a high-level abstract thought that leaves you frustrated. I will walk you through very specific items you can take to your home, community, and families in order to pull down walls of division. I ask questions throughout the paragraphs, not just at the end of the chapters. I challenge you to pause. Please take the time to reflect on the questions that challenge you. Develop a personal action plan before you move on to the next thought. That is how real change comes to our hearts and communities.

As I mentioned in the preface, I will provide my experience, which includes what I have experienced within my faith. While you may or may not be a person of any particular faith, I still invite you, welcome you, to walk through this journey with me and see through the eyes and footsteps of one who has walked on both sides of the lines of division and found a place of compassion and unity. I pray you will have an open heart and mind as you read this book.

I believe you will find ways to respond to the problems of division and racism that will provide hope and healing in your own life and in the lives of others.

Come take a walk with a half breed and find unity in a divided world.

# CHAPTER 1

# THE HALF BREED

**But God has shown me that I should not call
any man common or unclean.**

ACTS 10:28

I was born in 1980 in Seattle, Washington, to an African-American father and a first-generation German-American Caucasian mother. My dad was born in the South during the most segregated and prejudiced time in America. Both of his parents are black and were born and raised in Texas. My mom was born in Germany and moved to the United States when she was three. Her father was a Polish-American soldier stationed in Germany in the 1950s where he met and married my grandmother. I am mixed: half white and half black.

I am the oldest of four girls, and we all grew up knowing that even though our DNA was half white, our records and paperwork would likely still define us as black. I was aware of the "one drop" rule for blacks. Essentially, if you had one drop of black blood, you were defined, coded, and legally black. Both of my parents did a great job of making sure they reinforced that we were not just one or the other but both. A form would come home from school every year to verify personal information: address, birthdates, parental information, and race. My mom would intentionally handwrite "black/white" on our school forms under race. In the 1980s, there was not a "multiracial" or "mixed" box to check. The options were typically white, black, or Hispanic. The fact that we could only choose one made me feel like I had to identify with that one race. The system was forcing us to choose a side.

Despite my mom's best efforts, every year the school administration would edit the form and select black as our race. It stopped bothering us, eventually. *That was just how it is*, we told ourselves. Mom, however, would not allow it to stop her from intentionally correcting the paperwork each year. One year, my third sister's form was returned with the race listed as white. I recall us laughing until we cried because my sister was defined as white. We never had that option before. We had cracked the system! The school had finally not automatically chosen black. We just assumed our mom must have written "white/black" instead of "black/white" and they took the first option. I like to think that the school did not intend to label us.

My parents were intentional in raising us to embrace our biracial identity, but even as a child I recognized there was a racial difference. Television, coloring books, my toys, movies and advertising—in everything I saw, white skin was overly represented relative to the population ratio of whites to blacks.

I remember when I received my first African-American Barbie doll. I was seven. That Christmas I was with my dad's family, surrounded by black cousins, aunts, and uncles. As all girls do with their Barbie dolls, I undressed her for an outfit change. I stopped and stared at the naked black Barbie. I had never seen that before. I overheard a family member commenting on my awestruck expression and chuckling. I felt slightly ashamed, but in my little seven-year-old mind I wanted to defend myself and say, "I have never seen a *black* naked Barbie before and it looks odd to me. It's not my fault!" In the 1980s, most Cabbage Patch dolls and Barbies I saw were Caucasian, and that is what I inherently learned was cute or beautiful in the world's eyes. When I did see African-American dolls, they were not representative of most African-American skin tones, being much darker. It was not until I was nearing high school that dolls began appearing with multicultural skin tones that resembled me and my sisters.

My biracial family played a huge role in my personal understanding of both races, as well as my place within those races. I can trace my heritage past both sets of grandparents. I was fortunate to know my grandparents well, spending summers and holidays in their homes. Three of my four grandparents were in my life until I was thirty-six and knew both my boys very well. The exception was my African-American paternal grandfather who passed before my second son was born.

Both of my grandmothers are strong matriarchs in their families, who set the course and legacy in my life of overcoming obstacles. One raised fifteen black children in the midst of difficult racial divide in the South, and the other faced enemy soldiers to escape a divided Germany after World War II, eventually raising three white daughters in the United States.

## BIGMAMA

Bigmama—the name my entire family affectionately calls my paternal grandmother—is the pillar and matriarch of my dad's family. "Bigmama" is a popular name of endearment for a grandma in the African-American culture, particularly in the South. As a young child, in my mind, having the name "Bigmama" meant you were the strongest and bravest person in the world. My grandmother married my grandpa young and birthed fifteen children, although the first two passed away just months after birth. Together they have over forty-five grandchildren, fifty-five great-grandchildren, and at least five great-great-grandchildren (although this number continues to increase as you read this book).

Bigmama was born in 1932 and was raised out in the Texas countryside during very difficult times of racial hatred and segregation. She saw firsthand some of the most unjust police encounters in her small Texas town. Her own grandmother was born in slavery and was half Native American. No one knew what her actual age was when slavery ended, so she was given an estimated age of nine. Bigmama grew up aware of her grandmother's past and the hateful times of the present, so she built her family to be strong, to have courage, and to be brave.

Despite the oppressive social norms and laws of the prejudicial South, Bigmama endured and she didn't "take no mess," as my dad would say. In order to protect her children and their value, she stood up to racism. My second-born sister and I stayed with her many summers when we were young and experienced her boldness firsthand. I recall one story told of Bigmama when she was at the grocery store and a man thought it was appropriate to cut in front of her in the grocery line because he was white. Bigmama apparently took hold of his grocery cart and flung it across the aisle. She did not accept any attempt to devalue her life.

Bigmama ran her father's business, a local dance hall. The dance hall was built by Bigmama's daddy in 1948. He built the hall with his bare hands on a ten-acre plot of land in town, after he raised the necessary funds by picking cotton and pecans. He only had a third-grade education. The official name of the dance hall is Wright's Park, named after my great-grandpa Olton Wright, though we refer to it as the Park within the family. Bigmama was asked to run it at the age of sixteen and continued doing so for close to seventy years. Some may call it a juke joint, but it was so much more than that. The hall and the property were used frequently within the black community for a variety of events, from baseball and church services to family gatherings. On the weekends there were dances, concerts, and a club. BB King played there in his teenage years. It was once used on weekdays as a segregated school house.

Some of Bigmama's best memories were of the traveling negro-league baseball tournaments and the barbeques that would take place on the Wright Park property. On Sunday, church services would often be held under the oak trees. My dad's favorite childhood memories were of the Easter egg hunts held on the several acres of land surrounding the hall, where the community would bring in all kinds of animals, from ponies to peacocks and fish tanks. It was almost a mini zoo. As one of the only African-American dance halls in Texas, the Park was featured in the publication *Texas Dance Halls: History, Culture, and Community* by Gail Folkins. Today, the hall is no longer being used, and my father's dream is to one day fully restore what his grandfather built.

My grandpa—Bigmama's husband—spent time hunting with his boys, building homemade go-karts, and running up and down the football fields cheering for his sons. He had nine of them. His hands could build or fix anything. He taught me to never chew tobacco—unlike him—and to speak kindly of others. His African-American roots came from Fort Worth, Texas, as far as we knew. After retirement, my grandpa could be spotted on the front porch in that small country town, waving to all the passing neighbors with a smile on his face. He worked hard at the local muffler company where he was employed and retired after thirty years. That was the exact span of time Bigmama birthed all fifteen of her children.

My father is her oldest son and third child. He has two older sisters. As a businesswoman in the community and a member of the Methodist church, Bigmama was highly respected. What I learned from her is the value of standing up for myself and not allowing anyone to treat me differently because I carry black blood. She also showed me the value of serving others in spite of your own personal hardships. Due to the size of the family, every holiday dinner was held at the Park. There would easily be over sixty people, just within the immediate family, attending Thanksgiving dinner. However, Bigmama cooked enough to feed the entire town and would take to-go plates to her cousins and friends in the community who were too ill to attend the meal themselves. To this date, she makes the world's best sweet potato pie and potato salad.

## GRANDMA

From ages two to eight, I lived in Texas near Bigmama, where I was accustomed to using that term rather than "grandma." It meant the same thing to me. When I moved to Washington State, where my maternal grandmother lived, I naturally called her "Bigmama," catching her off guard. I do not think she had ever heard the term before. I guess she thought I was actually calling her a big mama. She politely asked my mom that we call her "Grandma" or "Oma" (since she was German). "Grandma" it was.

Grandma was born in eastern Germany in 1927. She experienced a traumatic childhood: she was only twelve years old when

WWII started. Her father was a forester and refused to join the Nazi forces. She witnessed as he was held hostage and eventually killed by Russian soldiers. At the age of sixteen she had to leave her home. Two years later, by the time she was eighteen, Hitler was found dead and WWII eventually came to an end.

My grandma is also a brave hero in my eyes. After the war, Germany was officially divided into East and West by the Soviet military. My grandma knew her legacy could not survive if she remained behind the border of East Germany. A Soviet soldier and EMT who was a friend of my grandmother, but an enemy of East Germany, smuggled her through the divided embankment. Russian soldiers discovered them and shot at the ambulance, but they escaped East Germany and the flying bullets. While my grandmother had gained freedom, she refused to leave her mother behind. She snuck back into East Germany, this time paying off the soldiers at the gate with high currency: cigarettes. She was able to get both herself and her mother safely back across the border.

Grandma eventually met my grandfather, an American soldier from Brooklyn, New York, who was stationed in Germany. His grandmother came through Ellis Island from Poland. Both his parents were deaf-mutes, but they died when he was just a toddler. He enlisted in the army at the age of seventeen and continued to serve all the way through Vietnam, retiring shortly after.

When my grandparents married, Germans were still considered possible terrorists. The American military refused to recognize their marriage for at least two years after they married because Grandma was considered an enemy of the state. Even after giving birth to their first child, they still refused to recognize the marriage. My mother and her oldest sister were born in Germany but moved to a military base in North Carolina when my mother was only three. My grandmother officially left her home country to give her children a future. She and my grandpa eventually retired in Olympia, Washington, near the Fort Lewis military base. My mother spent most of her late childhood in Olympia.

Grandma baked the best German and European meals. She had her own garden with herbs and spices and her home always smelled like a cottage in the woods of Germany. She would hang dried herbs from the ceiling beams, contributing to the wonderful aromas and the cottage-like feel. Her fireplace was perpetually filled with burning logs and the brick chimney was covered in original German china. She tilled and planted until her yard looked like a hidden forest in Narnia, with little stone paths, secret gnomes peeking out from behind flowers, and benches covered in moss. To me, the colorful garden was like a little piece of heaven.

She also loved to paint. My grandfather was a natural carpenter and would build wood furniture, clocks, and German figures for her to paint. While Grandma spoke English, she had a thick German accent even until she passed at the age of eighty-eight. I took German courses in school for three years, but I could never keep up with her. Nor could I ever seem to pronounce or comprehend the actual German locations, names, and titles she would share with me and my sisters. She, like my Bigmama, was a strong-willed woman.

It was very difficult for my grandma to share details of her life with us. There would be rare windows of time when she would open up and share freely. It was always on her time. When she did share with us, she sounded like a history book going back in time. I wish I spent more time recording her stories. As a family we have pieced together a timeline of different events and stories she shared, but it is still not as clear as we would like. Most of my life I did not understand why she was so hesitant to share her past with us until I visited the holocaust museum in Jerusalem, Israel, and understood the dark history of Germany that likely haunted her childhood memories.

Unfortunately, war, racism, and division are still experienced around the world every day. Although she didn't talk about it often, my grandmother demonstrated a powerful truth: when man tries to imprison you behind divided walls, continue to fight for freedom—yours and the freedom of others—even if it might cost you everything.

## MY PARENTS

Despite being a straight-A student in high school, on college fair day, my father, and the other black students, were pointed toward the army recruiting table while the white students were pointed toward colleges. At age seventeen, he enlisted in the army. As fate would have it, my father left a German-influenced Texas town, traveled through Germany, and eventually landed in Fort Lewis, Washington, where he met my German-American mother. Both my parents loved to dance, so they found each other on the dance floor at the military base. It was 1977 and, as they would tell you to this day, that era gave us the best music of all time. Afros, bell bottoms, and Earth, Wind and Fire marked the beginning of their relationship.

My parents were married in my grandparents' home in Olympia in 1979. They were blessed with their first, chubby, almost ten-pound baby girl in 1980. Over the next six years they gave birth to a total of four daughters. They were both the first in their families to marry outside their race and produce mixed, mulatto, biracial, interracial, multicultural, half-breed children. Ironically, my mother and her sisters, who are half German and half American, are not considered or defined as mixed or half breed.

The term "mulatto" specifically refers to a person of mixed white and black ancestry, especially a person with one white and one black parent. In a country proudly described as a melting pot, labels are most commonly placed on people of color. Even though my mother is more ethnically mixed than my father, socially she is just white. It doesn't seem to matter that she has German, Polish, French, Russian, and Irish blood.

My parents taught us to value our cultures equally, not preferring one over the other. My family loved music and dance—I guess it was officially in our blood, considering my grandma owned a dance hall and my parents met at one. Even in our musical choices we learned to value diversity. We listened to music spanning from Eric Clapton, the Ohio Players, and Madonna, to Al Green, Taylor Dayne, and Lisa Stansfield. We loved everything created from the 1970s to the 1990s. In fact, my parents danced to "our" music and we danced to theirs. On any given Saturday night, you could find the entire family doing the running man to Bobby Brown and singing at the top of our lungs. That did not bode well for those who lived in the apartment below ours at that time.

My parents also loved to eat and try different foods. My dad was born and raised in the country where he shot his own food, so he had eclectic taste. He told us about eating rabbit, squirrel, and even his pet lamb for dinner. My mom grew up on European-influenced cuisine. As a family, we ate everything from Chinese food and teriyaki to boxed macaroni and cheese and barbequed ribs. My dad made the best ribs I have ever tasted, made even better with my mom's mustard potato salad, baked beans, and pico de gallo on the side.

My parents educated me and my sisters on the history and reality of racism and prejudice in the United States and in their own life experiences. My mom taught me that while, to her knowledge, her ancestors did not have slaves, it was still everyone's responsibility to stand up and speak against prejudice and racism. Even though she was white, she was just as convicted by racism and stood against it as fiercely as my black father who experienced it firsthand. In fact, she had even more empathy knowing that her German heritage was not far removed from the horrific and murderous oppression of Jews during the Holocaust. My mother stands by my dad's side to this day as an advocate for justice. My father taught me not only to stick up for myself but also to be proud of who I am. He is proud to be black and I am proud to be half black. In his eyes, race is never an obstacle that can hold us back from our destiny. That is our reality.

## CHILDHOOD

When I was five years old, my parents attended a nondenominational church in Houston. It was there that they decided to dedicate their lives to the Christian faith and raise their children the same. When I was in the sixth grade in a suburb north of Seattle, we were invited to attend the local Baptist church. The Sunday school bus would pick up all the local children every Sunday and take us to church. We learned Scripture and hymns and gave our lives to Jesus almost every Sunday. I became the church bus secretary. I think this meant I counted the kids on the bus. It was during these critical years for me as a middle-schooler that I joined the youth group. In addition to my dad's strong biblical leadership within our home, youth group kept me from trying to be like all the cool kids at school—seeking to find an identity in temporary experiences. But more than anything, youth group taught me that God created me on purpose. I learned that my identity is not tethered to a label of my gender, skin color, or financial status. Despite what I saw in the world around me, I carried a deep sense of hope for my life—maybe even more so because I was uniquely a half breed.

I remember times in my youth when I was proud to be half black and thankful to be half white. It was as if I had the best of both worlds. I had "good" hair according to the black girls, and I had a "good" tan according to the white girls. Because I was a child in the 1980s, my naturally crazy curly hair fit the trends and was highly sought after by women who paid hundreds of dollars to perm their hair. Unfortunately, Mixed Chicks (multicultural natural and curly hair products) didn't exist back then. In fact, there weren't any products available for mixed people or really any kind of curly hair products like there are today. I had to make my own half-breed options. Like any good child of the eighties, I had big bangs and used my mom's Aqua Net hairspray to keep them in place. I would slick my hair back into a wet ponytail using my dad's Jerry Curl activator spray for the back. I had big stiff bangs, a hard helmet head, and a juicy, curly ponytail—the original mixed chick.

Other times I would mix conditioner—or even lotion—with water in a spray bottle to try to find the perfect mixture for my hair type. It is hard to imagine now, but there really were only white hair products that made my hair too dry, or black hair products that made my hair too greasy. My dad encouraged us to create our own hair products and look into marketing them one day. Had we followed his advice, we might have products sitting on the shelf next to Paul Mitchell today.

My parents taught me to love who I am and value each and every culture I represent, which allowed me to live life unhindered by oversensitivity or offense. I trusted before I doubted. Growing up, I was not aware of much racism against me personally. I am not saying there was none. There was. In fact, there were times on the playground when I fought or got into childish trouble because of racist comments. My sister and I were called the N-word or "Oreo" by white students. I remember being called a "brownie" by a neighbor boy in the midst of some heated backyard baseball game. That was right before I kicked him off of his bike and then reported it to his mother.

Because I was not looking for racism, or even expecting it, I gave people the benefit of the doubt when it occurred, and I did not hold onto grudges or let it affect me negatively long term. When I was nearing seventh grade, a classmate made fun of my mixed race. I was at the bus stop waiting in line for the school bus with the other kids. The girl from my class was standing there, super cute, wearing a jean jacket and a mini-skirt. Typical eighties outfit. She started making fun of me and then said out loud, with contempt in her voice, "She is *mixed*!" I was surrounded by my neighbors and friends I had known since elementary school. I remember feeling embarrassed, lonely, and ashamed in that moment.

Looking at it now, I understand that she was bullying me, though I never considered that until recently. The only person who came to my rescue was my school friend Sylvia, who was Korean. She stood by my side and told me to ignore the girl. The odd thing is, the bully was mixed-race too. She was half white and half black, just like me. Her skin was lighter than mine and she could have probably passed as white with her fair skin and loose curls.

Despite the shame I felt that day, I was quick to forgive her. What I later learned, after befriending her, is that she was raised by her single white mother and did not get to spend time with her black father. She did not have any close friends either. What she was taking out on me was intended for her absent father. She was lonely and seeking love. Despite her shaming me, I still befriended her and loved her for the short time we were friends until she moved again in her likely broken home. I learned from that situation that people who hate typically hate something within themselves.

## THE MELTING POT

The economy was in a bad spot in the 1980s. Unemployment topped 10 percent—the highest since the Great Depression—after the Federal Reserve inflicted a recession on the economy. My parents were trying to feed and clothe six people, four of them children. My dad also worked for Boeing, a company that would hire and lay off their employees what seemed like every three years. When the layoffs hit, we went through some humbling times while we relocated often in search of opportunity for our family.

I was two when the first layoff struck. My dad and I hit the road for my very first two-and-a-half-day road trip. I do not think car seats existed back then, but I was my dad's roll dog from Seattle down I-5, through California, and eventually I-10 into Houston. My mom and baby sister followed on a flight shortly after. We returned to my dad's home state and he found work in insurance, sales, and military aircraft. When I was five, we bought a house with a swimming pool in Houston. We were rich in my mind.

I attended kindergarten through second grade in Texas, first in Houston, then Greenville, and eventually in my Bigmama's town, Schulenburg. My friends mostly consisted of black kids who lived in the country and said "y'all." I had the fun opportunity of going to second grade with my cousins on my dad's side of the family. Because the town was so small, and our family was so big, there was a relative in nearly every grade at the school. I had aunts and uncles in high school and middle school, and cousins in my elementary class and at recess. I was in heaven. My uncles were the stars on the high school football team. I felt like *we* ran the school. Besides my sister, I was probably one of the only mixed students at the school. I knew it, but it did not matter to me. I had one drop of black blood, therefore I fit in like the rest.

While there, however, I was aware of the undertones of racism that still existed. Unfortunately, one time I got caught up in the ignorance. When I was eight, I remember going to the restroom with one of my black cousins and a white student came in. We turned around and both called her a "honkey" for no reason. Fortunately, we got in trouble and received detention. I do not recall learning that anywhere specifically, but I did understand there was racial tension within the small town. I also understood that we lived on the *other* side of the town.

In the summer before third grade, we moved back to Washington State. (This is when I called Grandma "Bigmama" with my country twang.) Being biracial in Seattle was not a big deal. In fact, Seattle had a large interracial marriage population. It seemed popular. With the military population, as well as immigrants from Japan, the Middle East, and parts of Africa, it too was a melting pot. My parents didn't stick out or have to explain themselves to coworkers, friends, or neighbors like they did in Houston. My dad tells me that in one particular black neighborhood in the inner city of Houston, referred to as Third Ward, the neighbors were convinced my mom was an undercover police officer since she was white. She stuck out like a sore thumb.

When we moved back to the Pacific Northwest, I initially stuck out as different, but not because of my race. I was no longer in the Texas countryside with cows, horses, and hunting dogs. I was in a small suburb north of Seattle, and I attended an all-white school, mixed with Korean and Vietnamese students. I was teased when I spoke because I sounded funny. I was reminded that "y'all" is not a real word (any Texan today would disagree). While searching for a permanent place to live, we resided in a motel. The worst thing about having mixed daughters is when you live in a one-bedroom motel and all four of them catch lice at school. We passed it back and forth to each other multiple times. With our huge lioness manes of hair, our poor mother probably used up all her sick time combing and washing out lice. I would have shaved our heads. I think I missed weeks of school trying to overcome the catastrophe.

By the early 1990s, I was attending middle school and had several friends who were also biracial. Black and white marriages resulting in mixed children were very common culturally, although we were still in the minority compared to the Caucasian population. Ironically, I did not see many all-black couples or marriages in the suburbs of western Washington. When I saw a black adult in a relationship, it was typically a biracial couple.

Due to the one-drop rule, my sisters and I knew we were still considered black, even in the racially blended Pacific Northwest. I would say, "I was one of only two black students in my class. And I am not even black." I lived in an apartment in one particular neighborhood for five years, until I was in eighth grade. I developed deep friendships from early elementary school onward. Rhea was white and my best friend in fourth grade. Glenda, from fifth grade, was mixed. In sixth grade I was friends with Tara Chan from Cambodia, Vivian from Vietnam, and Sylvia from Korea. In seventh and eighth grade, I became best friends with Kitaka Neal, my first black friend since Texas.

At the end of eighth grade, Boeing went through another massive layoff. We moved to Lake Charles, Louisiana, where my dad would work for the aircraft company Northrup Grumman. Louisiana is where I started high school. Washington and Louisiana are extremely different. I was convinced we were moving to swamps to live among alligators and I was not very happy about it.

Up to that point, I had lived among whites, blacks, mixed, and people from various Asian cultures. In Lake Charles, I was shocked to attend a magnet school that was 95 percent black. Strangely, I met kids who defined themselves as fully black, despite their red hair and freckles. They even had lighter skin than I did. I did not understand. Some even had blonde hair, blue eyes, and pale skin, and they believed they were 100 percent black. Initially, I was very confused.

I learned about Creoles, a mixed race stemming from French colonists and people from the Caribbean who settled in Louisiana decades ago. Over time, the intermingling of the races produced light-skinned black people, or white-skinned black people. Some of them were as white as my white mother, with hair even lighter than her brunette locks. The interesting part is that my black and Creole classmates did not believe my mother was white. They assumed, and believed, that I was just light skinned like them. When I told them my mother was white, I was met with prejudiced comments. Some of the black students could not believe a black man and white woman were married, as if it was not approved of even in 1995. While there was a large Creole population in Louisiana, it was still not as socially acceptable for a full black and a full white to marry. Biracial marriages had been accepted in Seattle since the 1970s.

I learned that prejudice still existed as much as it had when I was a young child in Texas, though maybe more in Louisiana. My sister Rianna had the same experience in her middle school. A boy saw my mother drop her off at school one day, and he made fun of her and embarrassed her in front of the class. From that day forward she was cautious of our mom dropping her off at school. Rather than being made fun of for speaking with a country accent, this time I was asked why I spoke "so proper," inferring I spoke like I was white.

In Louisiana, I found out I had a talent for running and I went to the 5A High School State Track Meet at LSU, placing second in every relay event with my teammates. I even met Carl Lewis there, an Olympic medalist. It was the beginning of a new journey and identity for me.

There were racial challenges in Louisiana, but I was also exposed to some beautiful cultural experiences. The food in Louisiana sent taste buds exploding into existence that had been dormant my entire life. I tasted dishes I had never heard of, let alone knew how to spell: crawfish, boudin, étouffée, jambalaya, andouille. I ate gumbo sometimes at Bigmama's house, but the rest of these dishes were foreign and amazing. Red beans and rice. Dirty rice. I had never eaten so well in my life.

While we fell in love with the food, zydeco music, and the Cajun people's tongue-twisting accent, our residence in Louisiana did not last long. Unfortunately, the economy was not good, and the education system was low performing. My dad could tell that staying there would affect our future. We moved back to Washington just as Boeing began another round of hiring.

When I moved back to Washington my sophomore year, I attended an all-white high school in Everett, a city about thirty minutes north of Seattle. I was considered the "black" girl by my senior year. I could count on one hand all the black students in all of the high school classes.

During my sophomore year, we lived in housing that was primarily filled with Russian, Middle Eastern, and Vietnamese families. We learned a lot about the different cultures, from clothing styles and car types to food and gender inequality. The Middle Eastern women would walk several feet behind the men on family walks, garbed in their native dress. The Russian men wore cool jumpsuits. They and the Vietnamese drove Hondas. Our next-door neighbors were Vietnamese and we became good friends with their families, often sharing food with one another. One day they brought us a dish that looked terrifying. It was yellow and slimy and looked disgusting to me, but it was a delicacy to them. We did not offend or ask questions. As an adult, I saw the fruit at a grocery store and was able to educate my friends about it so they would not freak out. Ironically, when we shared our potato salad and barbeque ribs with our Vietnamese neighbors, they gave back the potato salad. I assume the yellow mushed mess of slop looked disgusting to them as well. Go figure.

One day in my sophomore year, I entered my English class to find my teacher had placed my latest writing assignment on the overhead projector—without my permission—as an example of how *not* to write a paper. She, along with my classmates, picked at certain phrases and word choices and laughed together. I thought I would die in class that day. I received a D in that class that semester after earning an A in English in Louisiana freshman year. Apparently, there was a discrepancy in the education system. I did not learn how to really write a paper until my freshman year in college. I had a professor who took the time to help me understand the structure of writing an essay, and I started to fall in love with writing. I would love to share this book with the two of them. I wonder which one would be more surprised.

Though I was clearly in the minority at Everett High School, I graduated with a great experience. I played volleyball, basketball, and ran track, going to the State meet each year. I was friends with the jocks to the band kids, and everyone in between. I was in Student Body Council, president of the multicultural club, part of Youth and Government, and I was on the Homecoming Court senior year—all while taking honors classes. We attended a church down the street from my school, but I never went to the youth service. My sisters and I always sat in the adult services.

I walked onto the track team at the University of Washington, where I eventually earned a scholarship. My four years as a Husky athlete provided the most well-rounded experience for me. I found my community among the multicultural university athletes. I found myself feeling at home, initially, among the black athletes. I felt accepted and that I had found "my people." They understood my struggles as a minority—since I graduated from a predominantly white high school. But I was also reminded that I was not the same as the other black athletes.

My black friends affectionately referred to me as a "light bright." I saw and heard an undertone of judgment there but chose to laugh it off. It reminded me of my roots and that I was not black or white. I was neither. I was both. I was a mixed breed.

I found great friendships among my white and black teammates alike. Our 1600-meter relay placed third at the PAC-10 Championship and it consisted of two white girls, a mixed girl, and a black girl. USC and UCLA beat us by their noses at the finish line. Sports provide a great arena for unity among people of all different colors, creeds, and religions. My two roommates in college were also my closest friends and teammates. Shavon is black and Zee is half Belizean and half Panamanian. I was also close to a tall, white, lanky distance runner named Kara, whose wedding I was in after graduation. Cita, an intern I met in the summer before my senior year, became a lifelong friend. She is from Belize but looks like a light-skinned African American.

For the first time in my memory, men who were white, black, and any other race made it known I was attractive to them, something that never happened while I attended the all-white high school. I honestly did not think white men found black or mixed women attractive. While I dated an African American in college, as a child, I always thought I would marry someone like myself: mixed. Time would tell.

## EMBRACING DIVERSITY

Living in Texas, Washington, and Louisiana gave me insight into the three main political parties and how they each affected the communities where I lived. Louisiana was a Democratic state when I resided there and had been for about ten years. Texas was Republican, and while Washington was widely Democratic, there also existed a heavy Libertarian expression. We lived in every type of housing, including staying with family and friends, apartments, temporary housing, single-family houses—some with swimming pools, some without. I saw, and felt, the impacts of political agendas not only in my life but also in the lives of my neighbors and friends who shared those communities with me. We gained and lost from both sides. It was the best of times and the worst of times, depending on the times.

After my mom was laid off from Boeing, one political party supported her going back to school while the other passed legislation to remove the funding that would allow her to pursue an education. One party celebrated capital enterprise for motivated people, while the other flirted with encouraging laziness. After my dad taught us the truth of the Bible, I honestly found it impossible to be a pure

Democrat or a pure Republican. Both parties have great agendas, and both parties are missing the mark. Both have moral values. Both have forgotten God's heart. It was ironic to me, as a mixed person, that I would have to choose just one political affiliation. I was taught my entire life that one is not better than the other. Declaring Independent seemed the way to go. That seemed like the *mixed* option in my mind. I began to feel that strict political opinions were narrow-minded. We should love and help hurting people without crippling them, and reward and love hard-working people but not cripple them either. Once I reached voting age, I began exercising my rights to cast a mixed vote. I have voted Republican some years, Democrat other years, and sometimes I simply could not support either one.

After graduating college, I went on to work in the insurance industry, though my initial plan was to attend law school. That is a book for another day. It was there that I met my husband, James, who is also biracial.

His father was from New Orleans, a dark-skinned Creole with blue eyes. His mother is of Irish and Native American descent. Almost every one of my husband's siblings have a different eye color. In fact, his brother, who is ten months younger, has a daughter whose mother is white. Their daughter has blue eyes, blonde hair, and fair skin. She looks completely white. You would not know her dad is half black or that her grandpa is all black. James and I have two boys, Jalen and Noah. They are very mixed. They have different shades and texture of hair and different skin tones. My sister Rianna has three children, and they, too, have all different shades and texture of hair. Both of our oldest children are darker in tone while both of our second children have almost dirty-blonde hair and lighter skin. They are beautiful rainbows.

I had an emotional experience when my first child was born and it came time to define his race. Both of his parents are mixed. While the world typically defined me as black, I felt like I could not do the same thing to him. He had a right to be who God made him to be: a very culturally mixed child. He is not just black, as the paperwork would try to fashion him. It was such an odd dynamic. My husband and I knew we were not only black. We could try to resist the status quo and make life more difficult for others, or we could just go with the flow.

I was at work one day, talking to a black coworker who I had known since I was an intern in college. I worked with her for at least six years and I looked up to her because she trained me when I was in college. We shared personal life stories, and I considered us friends in addition to coworkers. That day the topic of interracial marriage came up. I was shocked when she blatantly said, "I don't believe black and white should mix to produce children." Obviously, she knew I was mixed. I was so confused in that moment. My heart heard her say, "I don't believe you should have been born. You should not be alive. Your life is not worthy of living." I was so hurt as I listened to her belittle my existence with her words, her feelings, her opinion, and her prejudice. She went on to complain that surely a white mother could never understand how to fix a mixed child's hair. That was primarily the basis of her argument.

Interestingly, my sons attend a private school now, where they are some of the only males of color. They are aware of it and joke that they are the only "black" kids, like I once did at their age. While our suburb may not be very diverse, my husband and I have created a family dynamic where our kids spend time with their black, white, and mixed cousins. We travel to Seattle often, as well as the Texas countryside. They run track, where most of their teammates are black, and they play golf, where most are not. They have played football, basketball, soccer, and baseball that have all brought them in contact with a beautiful mixture of cultures and people groups.

In January 2018, the Marvel box office hit *Blank Panther* was released. It made over a billion dollars worldwide, making it one of the highest-grossing films of all time. I was very joyful and emotional about this movie: a film that celebrates the strength, power, culture, colors, royalty, intelligence, and the land of the African people. What an announcement to the world of their value. To express such valor—and for black people to see themselves portrayed with such strength—honors their value. The film shows such an integrous, moral, and intelligent quality of life for black people of any nationality, a life that is not connected or limited to drugs, rap music, or sports. The film also celebrates the natural beauty and strength of women, emphasizing unity between men and women.

As a mother of young men of color, it was important to me for them to see their heritage with value, worth, and integrity. One of my sons told me a Caucasian friend commented a few times about how the movie had too many women and too many African characters for him to enjoy and identify with. He was not trying to be ugly. He was just not used to it and it was odd to him. I was not mad. It reminded me of the point: that women and African Americans were affirmed through a movie reflecting who God created them to be. It is important for us to have representation and role models in all industries, especially outside of just ESPN. That said, the greatest role models to my sons are not limited or defined by color or race alone.

When my husband and I moved to Dallas for work in 2002, we began looking for a church. It was important for us to belong to a church that reflects our family. We wanted to find somewhere multicultural. We were both used to eating sweet potato pie at one family gathering and pumpkin pie at another. We spend holidays with both our white families and our black families. We were not going to choose one over the other.

However, every church we walked into for the first six months was segregated. I doubt they were intentionally segregated. I just don't think they were intentionally integrated, either. As soon as we walked into a congregation, we could immediately tell if it was an all-white church or an all-black church. We attended Baptist and Methodist churches, and everywhere in between. We would get up on a Sunday and just drive until we saw a church and pull in. It was not until November 2002 that I was led to a specific church that my friend in Houston recommended. Ironically, the installation guy for our blinds had given us the name of this church six months prior, but I could not find it.

When I walked in that Sunday, I could not believe my eyes. Not only did the church represent every hue of the color wheel, but they were sitting next to each other! What caught my eye was an elderly white man sitting next to a young man from India. And they both were lifting their hands, worshiping together. There were hundreds of people in the sanctuary of every race all doing the same thing: worshiping their Creator. I do not remember the message. I do not remember the worship team. I do not remember if anyone spoke to me. I just remember that I saw heaven on Earth maybe for the first time in my life. I was coming back for sure.

I brought James the next Sunday. I did not have to tell him a single thing. He felt it, too. Four weeks later we became members and have been actively part of Covenant Church, in Carrollton, Texas, since January 2003. The pastor, Mike Hayes, wrote a book on racial reconciliation and has been traveling and speaking on that topic for several years. The story he shared with us is that in the 1990s, God put it on his heart that his church did not reflect heaven. It was all white. He became intentional about making it look the way it does today. At that time, he started to share his heart about unity among races in north Texas and he started to receive threats from the outside. In fact, an arsonist set his office on fire as a hate crime. At that point, it spiritually ignited the church with a passion to unify and strengthen the community.

Today, Covenant Church has over 12,000 members that represent nearly every culture, race, and color on the globe. It was not an accident. It was intentional. Pastor Mike Hayes has challenged me that we have to be intentional to unify. It does not happen coincidentally. Well-known pastors on TV have commented that the answer to our nation's division lies within Covenant Church, often recommending that more pastors speak to Mike Hayes.

Recently, the city where we live experienced an incident that showed up on national media and added to the racial tension in our country. The mayor and police chief both spoke to our local campus pastor, commenting that our church has the solution to the divides in our country right now.

The United States was founded on melting cultures together, yet we have somehow forgotten that. James and I took one of the DNA ancestry tests and found we have the following ancestry between us: French, German, Irish, British, Spanish, Greek, Portuguese, Native American, Indonesian, Nigerian, Ghanaian, Guinean, Congolese, and other sub-Saharan and western African DNA. I love what research is doing for our world now. We are finding out that we have nationalities within us that we never imagined, bridging gaps and bringing us all that much closer together. There are videos on social media of men and women finding out they hold the blood of the very nationalities they are admittedly prejudiced against. Ironically, the Jews and Samaritans shared the same blood through the fall of Israel, but they hated each other. This is the same all over the world. America is not the only country with race wars, but we can be part of the solution.

I was recently visiting a friend who decorated her beautiful home with a shabby chic décor. I was admiring this when I noticed she had a bushel of cotton in a vase. It was decoration. I honestly had not ever thought of using stems of cotton—like stems of hydrangea—to decorate my home. In fact, I had many emotions in that moment. I had to decide if I was offended that she would dare to decorate her home with something that scarred many of my ancestors, or if I should shake it off.

My great-great-grandmother's photo hangs at the Park. When I look at her stark and serious face, I think of cotton fields. It gives me shivers. It makes me sad. It makes me angry. It also makes me thankful that we do not live in that time. I decided at that moment that I could not allow a cotton bushel to define me. Categorize me. Shame me. Paralyze me. In fact, it would be a reminder of what God has brought my family through. He brought my family through slavery and gave them freedom. I recently purchased a bushel of cotton branches from a craft store and placed it next to a photo of my great-great-grandma. It is a reminder of the struggles she endured, and that I will never return to bondage as a slave—mentally, emotionally, physically, racially, or spiritually. I am free and I will use that freedom to help set others free.

When I reflect on my life as a person of mixed race, culture, financial status, religious denomination, and political affiliation, I realize that I am stronger because of it. A grafted branch is stronger than an original branch. The grafted tree builds up better resistance to disease and multiplies fruit much quicker. My dad told me once about the composite wings they made at Boeing for the newest airplanes. Composite is a mixture of metals and is stronger than pure metals. In the same way, I am better, stronger, because of my life experiences as a mixed breed. I have built up a resiliency to division and a desire for unity as a result of who I am. When I shared with my mother that I was going to write a book about division and being a half breed, she stoically reminded me that I was a whole breed. I have been given the opportunity to bring strength and wholeness to a divided breed, a divided nation.

The fact is, we are all grafted in—all part of the same tree. I believe that not one person is a mistake. God made me and He made you. White. Black. Pacific Islander. European. Asian. Indian. African. We are made in the image of God and He was intentional in making us the race—or races—that we are. The world seeks to remind us that we're different, wrong, that we don't fit in. We all belong, we all have a role to play, and it is time to embrace who we truly are.

# CHAPTER 2

# A DIVIDED NATION

**Every kingdom divided against itself is brought to desolation, and every city or house divided against itself will not stand.**

MATTHEW 12:25

Martin Luther King, Jr. led the March on Washington on August 28, 1963, in Washington, DC, delivering his life-changing "I Have a Dream" speech to our country. He stated:

1963 is not an end, but a beginning. And those who hope that the Negro needed to blow off steam and will now be content will have a rude awakening if the nation returns to business as usual. There will be neither rest nor tranquility in America until the Negro is granted his citizenship rights. The whirlwinds of revolt will continue to shake the foundations of our nation until the bright day of justice emerges.

He pointed out that justice, equality, and unity had to be officially dealt with or America would continue to be unstable. Unity cannot be a temporary or superficial fix but must be dealt with deep within the roots of our nation. Unfortunately, it appears the superficial bandages we placed on disunity and inequality have fallen off.

America has been plagued by a rise of ugly racial issues once again. Our country feels just as divided, hostile, and offensive today as it did in the height of the Jim Crow days. For some, it feels just as dangerous and uncaring. For others, it feels like excuses are being made and fingers are being pointed for life's hardships. One thing is sure: we have turned our backs on one another, despite who is at fault or in the wrong.

Martin Luther King, Jr. was a Baptist pastor and activist who led our country into the Civil Rights Movement. He is well known for his non-violent protests and for fighting against the discrimination of blacks. He was the most important voice in accomplishing the passing of the Civil Rights Act and Voting Rights Act for African Americans in the mid 1960s. Unfortunately, he was assassinated in 1968. The assignment he started was not finished.

The government got involved and led our country out of discrimination through rules, regulations, and laws. But that is where we fell short. The government does not control our hearts. Martin Luther King, Jr. preached his messages in the church; however, the church remains one of the most segregated places. The message of Martin Luther King, Jr., and of unjust equal rights, was shared and discussed, but did it penetrate the hearts of the very institution where unjust heart issues are addressed, confessed, and repented of?

## TAKE A STAND

In the last five years there has been an uptick in controversial violence involving black males and police officers. An international activist movement campaigning against violence and racism, called Black Lives Matter, started in 2013 as a response to these unjust acts of violence. A counter-movement, called Blue Lives Matter, was founded a year later, advocating for prosecution of those killing law enforcement officers in acts of hate crimes. In 2016, San Francisco 49ers quarterback Colin Kaepernick started a movement within the NFL that likely cost him his football career. He protested the recent shootings of minorities by not standing during the national anthem. In an interview with NFL.com, Colin shared, "I am not going to stand up to show pride for a flag for a country that oppresses black people and people of color. To me, this is bigger than football and it would be selfish on my part to look the other way."

Colin's protest spread throughout the NFL that season as well as into the 2017 season. It became a controversy among fans, family, and friends. Social media went haywire. Hatred, offense, prejudice, and ignorance had its finest hour in our country. Some teams would stand in unity. Some kneeled in unity. Some were mixed. Fans were angered that this issue was being brought into a game that they paid to watch. Players stood for their unnamed brothers who would never be seen on national television. The national anthem no longer played for the *United* States of America but the *divided* States of America.

Some of my family shared that while people said Colin was kneeling, they believed he in fact was standing. He was standing for what is right, the value of life, instead of kneeling or bowing for money and the safety of a paycheck, fame, and fortune. Colin was benched in November 2016 following a shoulder injury the prior season. His team had a losing season and a good reason to bench the quarterback—if that was in fact the real reason. The 49ers claim they were supportive of his efforts. Colin opted out of his contract in 2017 and had difficulty being picked up by another NFL team despite his Pro-bowl and Super Bowl appearances.

Discussions about this event came up in every space, including in work meetings, with coworkers, and around the dinner table. At first I avoided these discussions for the sake of unity; but over time, something inside of me began rising up. Sometimes the very things that bring unity come out of the most controversial discussions. Avoidance does not bring healing. It only provides a bandage, while the disease spreads unseen. Initially, I felt that I should just try to keep the peace. But peacekeepers don't make peace; peacemakers do. The kind of peace I was seeking, however, sometimes only comes after a war.

In August 2017, once the NFL season reheated the stand or kneel frenzy again, I turned my thoughts into a short essay called "I stand":

> To stand or sit is not the question. The better question is . . . why are they sitting? Even better question . . . does anyone really care?
>
> For men and women of faith, you know God gives you free will to choose Him, reject Him and even ignore Him. He does not force faith on you. It's called free will. It's a beautiful thing.
>
> America is great because of the same . . . free will. I am glad I live in a country where I can speak for, or against, my government and not be murdered. My free speech could

even be condemning, but that, again, is what makes our country great. Free will.

In fact, that is what our very great men and women of all races have fought for. They did not fight to force you to stand. They fought so that you could stand or sit depending on your own conviction. Therefore, it is not unpatriotic to stand or sit. What is unpatriotic is to ignore the injustices of the brothers and sisters, of all races, who also represent that same flag. Therefore, I stand for a flag I pray protects its people—not just yesterday, but also today and tomorrow—including my two young boys, so that they may sit (if they choose). God bless America.

The year 2017 was a year of catastrophic weather and events, with Hurricane Harvey in Houston and flooding in China and India. Hurricane Irma and Maria devastated Puerto Rico. Mexico had an earthquake, and Northern California caught fire, destroying thousands of acres and killing 111 people, with more fires scorching 280,000 acres in Southern California two months later. A typhoon caused one billion dollars in damage in Vietnam, and there were more earthquakes and even a volcano in other countries. Damages totaled close to 306 billion dollars. It was a devastating year. It was a scary year. The earth shook with fury. People started to question the times. Social media was full of devastation, sorrow, and fear. Discussions of racial tension just added to the fear and devastation, and our country was seized by political unrest as President Donald Trump was inaugurated in January 2017. Family members, coworkers, and friends started to unfriend each other on social media by the dozens over these controversial topics and alignments.

One day in late 2017, in the middle of a presentation, I shared my heart to make peace, not only for family and friends but also for my clients. What I shared with my coworkers is that no matter the chaos, the division, and the uncertainty in our country and in the marketplace, I would choose to be someone who brings calm. I would not add fuel to the fire on social media. I would not undermine the pain of any #livesmatter campaign. I would not contribute to the stress of a politically, socially, and spiritually divided country. I played a PowerPoint outlining all of the fires our country was currently undertaking in these areas, with the tune of "America the Beautiful," sung and recorded by Ray Charles, playing in the background. After I shared my heart to bring unity and calm to a place of division and storms, I looked around to find not one dry eye in the conference room.

This was something new developing within me. I was discovering a voice, my voice, that I had not previously heard or considered, or recognized. I started sharing my pastor's message on reconciliation with friends, particularly showing them a TBN interview with him and Dr. Bernice King, Dr. King's daughter. A friend called and thanked me for sharing the message. As a white male, he had not previously considered his role as an intentional reconciler. Now, he has welcomed it. He also shared that he believed I was a credible source since I was biracial, having the unified perspective of both black and white issues.

A year and a half after Kaepernick left the 49ers, in September 2018, Nike released a bone-chilling ad titled "Dream Crazy," narrated by Kaepernick and showing inspirational footage of impossible sports accomplishments. At one point, Colin looks at the camera and says, "Believe in something, even if it means sacrificing everything." The response to the commercial was explosive.

People burned their branded Nike gear in protest. President Trump chimed in on Twitter. I believe many people would agree with that statement, but few would have the courage to actually walk it out.

There is one man who lived with that level of courage, sacrificing everything, and He is the prime example for us all. His name is Jesus. Whether you are a follower of Jesus, agnostic, atheist, or somewhere in between, I challenge you to follow me from here. Our country is in a place of unrest and we need an answer before we implode. I believe that the life and ministry of Jesus Christ, written about in the Bible, has the answer for reconciliation of all people so that our country is once again fighting "until the bright day of justice emerges."

Justice, however, has been in the eye of the beholder. In our country, there are those who are ignorant to the pain, struggle, and oppressive history of their neighbors, a history that continues to plague them even today. Then there are those who are offended and unforgiving, allowing rejection to run so deep it borders on hatred and even reverse racism. If one side were to open a bridge of communication, grace, and understanding, then that would be a start. However, if the other side never walks across that bridge, then it is in vain.

Racism and hatred are not new phenomena. They run deep and wide and have an ugly resume of people groups they have tried to destroy since the beginning of time. Yet, there is hope for breaking these historical barriers—even here in America. Before we can understand the solution, however, we must first understand a two-thousand-year-old story about another divided nation, a half breed, and overcoming hatred.

## THE SAMARITAN HALF BREED

Prior to doing some research, I did not know much about the Samaritan people. They are real. They exist today. While in Israel, I learned that there is a small community there of approximately 300 Samaritans, although other sources say as many as 1,200 Samaritans live in the Middle East. Samaritans are referenced in the age-old phrase "good Samaritan," but for the complete opposite reason than you might expect. It is vital to understand who the Samaritan people are—and were—in order to see how the parable of the good Samaritan is part of the solution we need in our country today.

It starts with their racial DNA. King David, a beloved king and ruler of the nation of Israel, was succeeded by his son Solomon. Solomon's reign lasted forty years, and the land and people resided in peace under his leadership during this time. After King Solomon's death, the northern tribes revolted, dividing Israel into two separate nations: Israel in the north, and Judah to the south. Kings of both lands continuously fought each other until both were eventually taken into captivity.

The sixth king of Israel, Omri, purchased the land that was eventually named Samaria. First Kings 16:24 says, "And he bought the hill of Samaria from Shemer for two talents of silver; then he built on the hill, and called the name of the city which he built, Samaria, after the name of Shemer, owner of the hill." Omri established the area of Samaria as the new capital city that he completely controlled at the top of a hill, making it easy to defend. He reigned for twelve years and then passed the kingdom to his son Ahab. Ahab married the infamously evil queen Jezebel, and they built an altar and temple for the pagan god Baal in Samaria, leading the people into idol worship. Samaria served as the capital city for the rest of Israel's dynasty until it fell to the Assyrians.

The Assyrians resettled Samaria with their own people, forcing the ten northern tribes of Israel to scatter across the kingdom. Assyria's resettlement policy, moving the foreigners in and dispersing the Israeli captives, prevented the Israelites from uniting and revolting. Second Kings 17:24 says, "Then the king of Assyria brought *people* from Babylon, Cuthah, Ava, Hamath, and from Sepharvaim, and placed *them* in the cities of Samaria, instead of the children of Israel; and they took possession of Samaria and dwelt in its cities." Those Hebrews left behind in Samaria were of the lowest classes. They fragmented, intermingled, and eventually formed a new race, a half breed: the Samaritans. The Samaritans became the despised race, a polluted population of foreigners who took over the land, creating a new people and culture.

The Samaritans were given a priest to teach them about God. However, 2 Kings 17:33 and 40 say, "They feared the LORD, yet served their own gods—according to the rituals of the nations from among whom they were carried away. . . . However, they did not obey, but they followed their former rituals." These rituals included godless forms of idolatry, as well as sacrifice of their children. They were despised by full-blooded Hebrews even until the time of Christ.

Eventually, the southern territory of Judah was exiled to Babylon, leaving the divided nation of Israel further torn apart. The tribes of Judah, however, were not dispersed, allowing them to retain their culture and heritage even in exile. The Hebrew captives in Babylon were finally allowed to return to Jerusalem to rebuild the temple that had been destroyed in captivity. It was the people of Judah who returned to Jerusalem, while the ten tribes of Israel remained fragmented from the Assyrian captivity.

During this time, divisions only deepened between Hebrews and Samaritans. It was customary at that time that if the Hebrew people could not trace their heritage back to Abraham, they were not considered true Jews and were excluded from participation in Jewish community and traditions. Josephus, a Jewish historian, described the Samaritans as opportunists, wanting to acknowledge their blood relationships when the Jews enjoyed prosperity, but who disowned their kinship when Jews suffered hard times. The book of Ezra describes that when Jews from Babylon, led by Zerubbabel, went to rebuild the temple, the Samaritans offered to help. The Jews refused and so the Samaritans tried to sabotage the rebuild. Nehemiah was also opposed by Arab and Samaritan groups when he attempted to rebuild the wall in Jerusalem. Ezra demanded 113 families to divorce their "pagan" Samaritan wives. The final break between the two groups occurred after the Samaritans built a rival temple on Mount Gerizim, claiming Shechem rather than Zion (Jerusalem) as the true house of God. Samaritans celebrate Passover in Shechem even to this day.

In the time of Jesus, the territory of Israel was divided into three regions: Galilee in the north, Samaria in the middle, and Judea in the south. Situated between Galilee and Judea, Samaria was the natural route for traveling between the two territories. However, because pure-blooded Jews had no dealings with the Samaritans, they would travel east, cross the Jordan river, and detour around Samaria. Except for Jesus. He insisted on traveling through Samaria. While man tries to divide, Jesus unites.

The Bible is pretty clear about the disgust, hatred, and enmity between pure-blooded Jews and the Samaritans, due to racial, cultural, and religious differences. One may use this text within Scripture to propose that God is against intermarriage or mixing of races. That is not so. God's words were that believers are not to marry *un*believers, as it causes disunity in faith and in the home. Even

Ruth, the grandmother of King David, was not Jewish but from Moab (present-day Jordan). Unfortunately, many deceptive rulers in the past and even today will use the Bible to support racism, anti-Semitism, and oppression.

These issues of division and racism are still alive today. African Americans can identify with the Samaritan half breed. They are not completely African; however, they are also not native to America. Like the Samaritans, they were intermingled among other races against their own free will. Initially, they did not feel like they belonged. They were rejected by other races. What race of people has been largely trafficked and then recovered from that experience? What race, culture, or people group, after being exploited, stolen, raped, and destroyed, was able to turn around and see themselves as valued, empowered, loved, and worthy? What does slavery do to a nation? It steals, kills, and destroys worth, will, and value.

God's plan is quite the opposite.

# CHAPTER 3

# RECONCILER

**Now all things are of God, who has reconciled us to Himself through Jesus Christ, and has given us the ministry of reconciliation, that is, that God was in Christ reconciling the world to Himself, not imputing their trespasses to them, and has committed to us the word of reconciliation.**

2 CORINTHIANS 5:18-19

A long time ago in Israel, a man named Jesus stood up in a synagogue to teach from the ancient scrolls of a man named Isaiah. (Isaiah is considered a prophet in both the Jewish and Christian faith. Some of these ancient scrolls were found as part of the Dead Sea scrolls, and I saw them with my own eyes while in Israel.) When Jesus was finished reading the well-known passage, He sat down and spoke aloud for all to hear: "The Scripture you've just heard has been fulfilled this very day!" (Luke 4:20 NLT).

What He quoted was what we now refer to as the book of Isaiah, found in the Old Testament of the Bible. The passage is from chapter 61, but the story of Jesus reading the passage is found in Luke 4:18-19:

The Spirit of the LORD is upon Me, because He has anointed
Me to preach the gospel to the poor; He has sent Me to heal
the brokenhearted, to proclaim liberty to the captives and
recovery of sight to the blind, to set at liberty those who are
oppressed; to proclaim the acceptable year of the LORD.

Jesus came to set captives free in every way. Free from mental
captivity. Free from physical oppression. Free from spiritual dam-
nation. He is the ultimate reconciler. Anyone who says that Jesus is
the "white man's religion" has, unfortunately, experienced just that:
religion. Not Jesus. Religion controls and contorts, and it distracts
us from the truth. Jesus was not white. Jesus was not black. He was
born into a Jewish family so that God could fulfill His plan to bring
salvation to the whole world through the Israelites, the people with
whom He made a covenant promise.

Martin Luther King, Jr. believed and preached the gospel of Jesus. It was that very gospel that gave Dr. King the faith and courage to fight against injustice. It is the very gospel that gave him
the strength to lead in love through peaceful protests rather than
through violence driven by unrighteous anger. The gospel of Jesus
is what broke the chains of slavery in America and every form of
slavery across the globe. The gospel is love, and love seeks to serve
others and find unity.

This is seen clearly in the book of John, in the New Testament,
where the author shares a story that doesn't appear in any other
gospel. John is known as the beloved disciple, and I believe he wanted the reader to see themselves as beloved as well, including the
downtrodden and outcast Samaritan, who in this example is also
a woman. Women in the time of Jesus had limited rights and were
often even restricted by ceremonial laws. When allowed in pub-

lic, women were double veiled. They had little or no authority and were considered inferior to men. They were not allowed to testify in court. They were not allowed to speak to strangers. A married woman required permission from her husband to leave her home, and an unmarried woman required permission from her father. The Samaritan woman in John's story broke all of these rules. And then she encountered Jesus.

In John 4, he tells us that Jesus was ministering in Judea when some news caused Him to go back to Galilee. Instead of walking around Samaria, like so many others would in that day, He decided to pass directly through the tainted region. While there, He encountered a Samaritan woman, the one who broke the rules. He, too, broke the rules by having a conversation with her and, eventually, offering her eternal life.

> But He needed to go through Samaria. So He came to a city of Samaria which is called Sychar, near the plot of ground that Jacob gave to his son Joseph. Now Jacob's well was there. Jesus therefore, being wearied from *His* journey, sat thus by the well. It was about the sixth hour. A woman of Samaria came to draw water. Jesus said to her, "Give Me a drink." For His disciples had gone away into the city to buy food. Then the woman of Samaria said to Him, "How is it that You, being a Jew, ask a drink from me, a Samaritan woman?" For Jews have no dealings with Samaritans. Jesus answered and said to her, "If you knew the gift of God, and who it is who says to you, 'Give Me a drink,' you would have asked Him, and He would have given you living water." The woman said to Him, "Sir, You have nothing to draw with, and the well is deep. Where then do You get that living water? Are

You greater than our father Jacob, who gave us the well, and drank from it himself, as well as his sons and his livestock?" Jesus answered and said to her, "Whoever drinks of this water will thirst again, but whoever drinks of the water that I shall give him will never thirst. But the water that I shall give him will become in him a fountain of water springing up into everlasting life."

John 4:4-14

Despite the racial lines and boundaries that men put into place, Jesus intentionally walked through Samaria on his way to Galilee. He intentionally sought after the mistreated, offended, and oppressed. In the New King James Version of the Bible, John 4:4 says, "But He *needed* to go through Samaria" (emphasis added). The New International Version, and most other translations say, "Now he had to go through Samaria." But my favorite version is the Amplified Bible Classic Edition, which reads, "It was *necessary* for Him to go through Samaria" (emphasis added). He needed to go because He had a necessary assignment. He went looking for the one person who would bring an entire hated race to Him for salvation through her testimony. Jesus reconciled a nation by destroying all judgment, condemnation, offense, and prejudice.

It appears to us that Jesus and the Samaritan woman simply had a conversation. However, Jesus did more than destroy racism with His words. He destroyed racism through action. He did something about it. It's not enough for any one of us to say, "I am not prejudiced." We must also live from that place of acceptance and love. Jesus went into Samaria. He acted. He did what no other Jew would do in that time and went out of the way to befriend and encourage someone of a different race. He interacted with a Samaritan.

Jesus met the Samaritan woman in her world, at her well. That well was likely a very shameful and sorrowful place for her. Wells were commonly where women met their husbands. Women also customarily went to the well together. The Samaritan woman went alone in the hottest part of the day so no one would likely see her. Jesus sat with someone He was not supposed to be sitting with, mostly because she was a woman, but also because she did not meet the standard to converse with Him. John 4:9 points out her surprise, saying, "How is it that You, being a Jew, ask a drink from me, a Samaritan woman? For Jews have no dealings with Samaritans."

Being a young woman of color, I can identify with the Samaritan woman. I also often felt that I did not meet the standard, especially in the workplace where I was typically outnumbered by men. I work in an industry that is dominated by white males over the age of fifty. It was easy to feel I was not good enough when I looked around at my environment. However, I had to remember that Jesus intentionally seeks after me, pursues me, and loves me. After all, He created me.

Further in the story, we find that even the disciples are caught off guard by Jesus' actions. In John 4:27, it reads, "And at this point His disciples came, and they marveled that He talked with a woman; yet no one said, 'What do You seek?' or, 'Why are You talking with her?'" They wonder at His behavior, even though they do not say anything to Jesus. Good, godly people, disciples, even leaders and pastors can miss the heart of God and have prejudices that have gone unchecked. The disciples were not willing to say anything to Jesus, but they questioned Him in their hearts. The reality is, we all likely have some type of prejudices that we need to face. Who would the "woman at the well" be in today's society? What would she look like? What would be her race, socioeconomic class, political choice, or denomination? How would you or I perceive a woman who broke the rules? Your rules, my rules, rules that create separation, division, and exclusion. How might we judge her?

Our country is currently dealing with major division, offenses, and social injustices. How we choose to interact with others can either reconcile difference or add to the division. How do we deal with division and social injustice when we see it? How will you choose to bring healing to our nation and its people? Do you ever make fun of different accents or complain about the smell of another's food? Do you make biased assumptions of another's education or financial decisions, or mock music, culture, or rituals you are not accustomed to?

Many times these things are not intentional, but it does not make them any less prejudicial. We all need to check our hearts for prejudice and judgment. The best way I know how to do this is to ask God to examine my heart. King David wrote in Psalm 139:23, "Search me, O God, and know my heart; try me, and know my anxieties." In Psalm 51:10, after realizing his sin, he wrote, "Create in me a clean heart, O God." We serve a graceful God who is willing to forgive our shortcomings that we confess, including our prejudices.

My favorite part of this story is the salvation and reconciliation of a nation that is racially opposed to Jesus at the very end of the passage. Because Jesus prophesies about her life situation, the woman at the well knows there is something special about Him. She runs to tell the town about Him, claiming that He is Christ. John 4:40-42 says:

> So when the Samaritans had come to Him, they urged Him to stay with them; and He stayed there two days. And many more believed because of His own word. Then they said

to the woman, "Now we believe, not because of what you said, for we ourselves have heard *Him* and we know that this is indeed the Christ, *the Savior of the world*" (emphasis added).

I want to jump out of my skin at this declaration! Because Jesus showed up, and because a wounded woman of the wrong race was willing to lay aside her offense, a door was opened for her people to be set free.

Dear person who has been judged or oppressed based on color, race, culture, finances, ethnicity, or gender: come, taste and see the love of Jesus for yourself. Come and *know* He is the savior—of you, your family, and the world. He can heal all oppression, all racial offenses and bondage against you and the generations before you. Did you know you don't need to meet the approval of other races to be whole? You don't need the approval of others to know who you are, to be secure, content, and confident for your soul.

Dear person who has judged and oppressed others: have you failed to use your power, authority, and gifts to help fight against discrimination? Jesus is the savior of the whole world, not you alone. Jesus' grace and forgiveness are sufficient for all—all people, races, genders, and socioeconomic statuses—including you.

Are you willing to interact with people who are different from you? Will you choose to sit at a different table, go to a different gym, barber shop, or the other side of town? Are you willing to go out of your way, like Jesus did, to support your words and walk in an unfamiliar or uncomfortable situation?

There is nothing that holds Jesus back from us. He is the ultimate reconciler and He gives us the ability—and responsibility—to reconcile with others.

## JESUS EXPERIENCES DISCRIMINATION

In the book of Luke, one chapter prior to Jesus' teaching on the good Samaritan, we read that He and His disciples were refused housing in a Samaritan village on the way to Jerusalem. Just prior to this, Jesus had an experience on a mountain where He was transfigured and appeared to shine radiantly, like the sun. God spoke and affirmed Him in His resurrection assignment (see Matthew 17:1-13). As He and His disciples passed through the Samaritan village, He was on His way to face His destiny: to set captives free. The local Samaritans, however, would not allow them to stay because they were Jewish. The disciples were so angry at the rejection that they planned to retaliate with violence.

> Now it came to pass, when the time had come for Him to be received up, that He steadfastly set His face to go to Jerusalem, and sent messengers before His face. And as they went, they entered a village of the Samaritans, to prepare for Him. But they did not receive Him, because His face was set for the journey to Jerusalem. And when His disciples James and John saw this, they said, "Lord, do You want us to command fire to come down from heaven and consume them, just as Elijah did?" But He turned and rebuked them, and said, "You do not know what manner of spirit you are of. For the Son of Man did not come to destroy men's lives but to save them." And they went to another village.
>
> Luke 9:51-56

Like the disciples, have you ever been tempted to use your authority or power to control or manipulate someone who does not agree with you or has a different status politically, socially, financially, or theologically? The Jewish men were not only rejected, but they were also racially discriminated against by the people in that Samaritan town. They were rejected because of their blood, their nationality, their culture, and their religion. Today, we would call this social injustice. The disciples were so offended that they were tempted to use their authority to harm the Samaritans in return. Jesus reprimanded the disciples, reminding them what His purpose was, and what it was not. To bless and not curse. To lift up, not tear down. To include, not exclude. To save and not destroy. God established social justice. It was not established by activists or a certain political party. It was God's idea, and He demonstrated it through Jesus.

Leviticus, in the Old Testament of the Bible, outlines the moral laws around social justice. In Leviticus 19, God clearly commanded us to love others.

> And the LORD spoke to Moses, saying, "Speak to all the congregation of the children of Israel, and say to them: 'You shall be holy, for I the LORD your God am holy.... When you reap the harvest of your land, you shall not wholly reap the corners of your field, nor shall you gather the gleanings of your harvest. And you shall not glean your vineyard, nor shall you gather every grape of your vineyard; you shall leave them for the poor and the stranger: I am the LORD your God. You shall not steal, nor deal falsely, nor lie to one another. And you shall not swear by My name falsely, nor shall you profane the name of your God: I am the LORD. You shall not cheat your neighbor, nor rob him. The wages of him who is hired shall not remain with you all night until morning.

You shall not curse the deaf, nor put a stumbling block before the blind, but shall fear your God: I am the LORD. You shall do no injustice in judgment. You shall not be partial to the poor, nor honor the person of the mighty. In righteousness you shall judge your neighbor. You shall not go about as a talebearer among your people; nor shall you take a stand against the life of your neighbor: I am the LORD. You shall not hate your brother in your heart. You shall surely rebuke your neighbor, and not bear sin because of him. You shall not take vengeance, nor bear any grudge against the children of your people, but you shall love your neighbor as yourself: I am the LORD.'"

Leviticus 19:1-2; 9-18

Jesus quoted that very same Scripture in Matthew 22:37-40, declaring it to be one of the greatest commandments. The Scripture is clear that social injustice is wrong and should not be tolerated. Discrimination against another because of their financial status or physical limitations breaks God's law. He demands that we care for others, especially those who are taken advantage of.

Due to generations of injustice, offense, and hatred, the people of that Samaritan village allowed their own pain to grant division and prevent Jesus from reconciling their lives, families, and communities. Imagine what might have happened if that town had allowed Jesus to heal their wounds and offenses. He was on His way to Jerusalem to complete His mission, to save lives, and they let Him pass right by them. What might He have done for their hearts, minds, and souls? How might His ministry have impacted their children and their legacy? I can only imagine the healing that could have taken place: the refuge, the restitution, and the redemption.

Like the Samaritans, what past pain, hurt, and injustices in your life are you holding onto? What offense or discrimination is more important than receiving healing and unity in your heart? Jesus Christ holds no prejudices, and neither should we. There is one race He cares about: the human race.

Have you forgiven those who have hurt, offended, or oppressed you? What authority, power, or gifts do you carry that can be used to bring reconciliation—or division? Are you willing to use those gifts to restore relationships, cities, churches, or countries? Like Jesus, we also have the ministry of reconciliation of *all* people, whether Jew, Gentile, rich, poor, man, or woman. We have also been presented with the same challenge, or opportunity, as the Samaritan half breed: we can choose to be a victim, a survivor, or a reconciler.

# CHAPTER 4

# THE GOOD SAMARITAN

*Beloved, let us love one another, for love is of God; and everyone who loves is born of God and knows God.*

1 JOHN 4:7

A parable is a simple story that communicates a moral lesson, religious principal, or spiritual truth. The Greek word for "parable" means "a laying by the side of" or "a casting alongside." It is a comparison of something in order to place light on the other. Jesus told many parables in Scripture that were typically meant to enlighten those who sought truth and to blind those who did not. The parable of the good Samaritan is one of the most well known. "Good Samaritan" is also a term used in current culture to describe a person who selflessly helps another, especially someone in distress. There are even Good Samaritan laws today that provide legal protection from liability if consequences result from offering assistance to someone who is injured or in danger.

The parable illustrates God's love and His command to have compassion for all people. If we are honest with ourselves, we can relate to any one of the characters described in this story. Our ability to relate to their attitudes will reveal our true hearts and who we truly believe is our neighbor. Prepare to be enlightened.

And behold, a certain lawyer stood up and tested Him, saying, "Teacher, what shall I do to inherit eternal life?" He said to him, "What is written in the law? What is your reading of it?" So he answered and said, "'You shall love the LORD your God with all your heart, with all your soul, with all your strength, and with all your mind,' and 'your neighbor as yourself.'" And He said to him, "You have answered rightly; do this and you will live." But he, wanting to justify himself, said to Jesus, "And who is my neighbor?"

Then Jesus answered and said: "A certain man went down from Jerusalem to Jericho, and fell among thieves, who stripped him of his clothing, wounded him, and departed, leaving him half dead. Now by chance a certain priest came down that road. And when he saw him, he passed by on the other side. Likewise a Levite, when he arrived at the place, came and looked, and passed by on the other side. But a certain Samaritan, as he journeyed, came where he was. And when he saw him, he had compassion. So he went to him and bandaged his wounds, pouring on oil and wine; and he set him on his own animal, brought him to an inn, and took care of him. On the next day, when he departed, he took out two denarii, gave them to the innkeeper, and said to him, 'Take care of him; and whatever more you spend, when I come again, I will repay you.' So which of these three do you think was neighbor to him who fell among the thieves?"

And he said, "He who showed mercy on him." Then Jesus said to him, "Go and do likewise."

Luke 10:25-37

This parable is the answer to racial reconciliation. It is also the answer to gender, economic, and religious division. There are so many lessons to be learned within this passage. In order to truly understand what Jesus is sharing with us, it helps to review the passage by each character and their response. With an honest examination of our hearts, we should be able to see ourselves within each of them. And maybe, for the first time, we can learn to understand the perspective of another. That is where reconciliation begins.

## THE LAWYER

We have established that God's moral law, in Leviticus 19:18, is to "love your neighbor as yourself." What does love *really* look like? Whether you have never read the Bible, or you proclaim the faith of Christianity, you might suggest this is an easy answer. You might be surprised. The lawyer in our parable was an expert in the Torah. He knew the requirements of the law in Leviticus. But what was Jesus really asking him? Jesus wanted to know his heart, not his knowledge.

And behold, a certain lawyer stood up and tested Him, saying, "Teacher, what shall I do to inherit eternal life?" He said to him, "What is written in the law? What is your reading of it?" So he answered and said, "'You shall love the LORD your God with all your heart, with all your soul, with all your strength, and with all your mind,' and 'your neighbor as yourself.'"

Luke 10:25-27

The lawyer was correctly quoting Deuteronomy 6:5 but only partially quoting Leviticus 19:18. What is ironic here is that he left out an important part of the Scripture: "You shall not take vengeance, nor bear any grudge against the children of your people, but you shall love your neighbor as yourself: I *am* the Lord."

In Luke 10:28, Jesus tells the lawyer that his answer is correct, but He adds an unexpected response: "And He said to him, 'You have answered rightly; do this and you will live.'" Jesus told him to *do*—not think, study, or read scripture, but *do*. It is an action word, a verb. Love is also an action, not just a thought or an emotion. Jesus wants us to actively love God and other people; He wants us to live a life that is pleasing to God. Jesus told the lawyer, "do this and you will live." What was it he was meant to do? Love.

The English language has one word for love whereas the Greek language has several. It is difficult to understand which meaning of love is being referred to unless you reference the Greek or Hebrew translation. The three most popularly spoken or written are *phileo, eros*, and *agape*. It is very important to understand the biblical definition of love. Culture is subject to change over time, bringing forth differing opinions and philosophical, political, and social agendas. God's Word, however, is constant through time (see Malachi 3:6).

Phileo love refers to friendly love. Eros is erotic love. These are both conditional versions of love. They respond to giving and receiving. Eros is the lowest level of love as it is self-satisfying, depends on attraction, and may turn bitter.

Agape love is the greatest and noblest of them all. Agape is God's given nature. First John 4:8 says, "God is love." This love is the highest esteem that God has for His children and the high regard that we, in turn, should have for Him—and other people. God's love is everlasting, sacrificial, and free (see Jeremiah 31:3; Hosea 14:4; John 3:16). So, how do we love like God loves?

Paul defines agape love for us in the New Testament in 1 Corinthians 13:4-7. The Message version sweetly outlines it:

> Love never gives up. Love cares more for others than for self. Love doesn't want what it doesn't have. Love doesn't strut, doesn't have a swelled head, doesn't force itself on others, isn't always "me first," doesn't fly off the handle, doesn't keep score of the sins of others, doesn't revel when others grovel, takes pleasure in the flowering of truth, puts up with anything, trusts God always, always looks for the best, never looks back, but keeps going to the end.

It's easy to ramble off each of these, but I recommend you take the time to dissect each line against your heart. What does a love like this look like within your marriage, your work environment, at church, or in your extended family? How do you show this type of love to people in the *other* political party, spokespersons of social issues, a different religious denomination? What kind of *action* do you need to put forward in displaying love in *that* situation or toward *that* person within a different race, political party, or socioeconomic status? Real love is hard work and intentional. Unfortunately, the simple answer—to love your neighbor—was not enough for the intelligent lawyer. "But he, wanting to justify himself, said to Jesus, 'And who is my neighbor?'" (Luke 10:29).

The lawyer had no intention of being inclusive. He tried, instead, to limit, restrict, and exclude who he should consider as his neighbor. The lawyer was essentially asking, "Who do I *not* have to love?" His heart was truly revealed in that moment. If you ask yourself the same question, what does it reveal about your heart? Who is your neighbor? Which neighbor have you excluded or overlooked? Who do you need to intentionally love, as outlined in 1 Corinthians? You may need to stop and think about this for a moment. Consider praying that God brings that person, or people group, to your mind. If you cannot think of anyone now, do not be surprised if you think of someone as we continue through the parable.

## THE THIEVES

As the parable unfolds, Jesus educates the educated. This is where the divided history of Samaria, the lineage of discrimination, and the hatred of the half breed comes into the story. The half breed united a divided world even more than society's most powerful and influential leaders. Based on Jesus' audience, we can assume that the man violated by the robbers was of Jewish descent, which would have made him relatable to the lawyer and those listening. They could identify with his race, his gender, his socioeconomics, and his religion—which also meant they understood his convictions because they likely had the same convictions, good or bad.

> Then Jesus answered and said: "A certain man went down from Jerusalem to Jericho, and fell among thieves, who stripped him of his clothing, wounded him, and departed, leaving him half dead."
>
> Luke 10:30

The thieves had robbed this man of his identity, his dignity, his honor, and his provision. They left him to die, showing the world they had no compassion for his life or soul. They wished him dead.

They did not consider his family, wife, or children, or what condition this might leave them in without him providing for their home. They did not consider in what condition it might leave his community or his legacy. Most of us likely do not seek to kill or destroy another's life as described here. However, Jesus challenges us that what we believe in our hearts is just as bad as the crime itself. In the book of Matthew, He suggests that if you lust, you have committed adultery. If you hate, you have murdered in your heart.

This begs the question of what is truly in our hearts. Do we stop and think about the repercussions of a man, a community, or a nation that is left to die? Do we care about how our actions impact the world around us? Are we the thieves, destroying the identity of our neighbors and our nation? When you see an injustice; a crime; an offense; an attempt to destroy a life, a people group, or a reputation, how does your heart respond? What does your response lead you to do?

## THE PRIEST

> Now by chance a certain priest came down that road. And when he saw him, he passed by on the other side.
>
> Luke 10:31

Priests were descendants of Aaron, the original High Priest with Moses, and were ordained to serve as official ministers and leaders in the nation of Israel. The priests represented the highest level of moral integrity. They represented God to the people and represented the people before God. The priest would enter God's presence—after a process of purification—and conduct offerings so that sin might be forgiven. They were meant to lead by example and teach the people how to distinguish between holy and unholy, clean and unclean. Even the priest's clothes had great significance of holiness, spiritual integrity, and righteousness. Only the priest could enter God's presence at the temple to speak on behalf of the people and intercede for their salvation, restoration, and forgiveness.

Unfortunately, the priest in the parable did not bother to assist the injured man. He simply passed by on the other side of the road when he saw him from a distance. He avoided him. He didn't even try to get a closer view of the situation. Perhaps the priest was too holy. Perhaps he was so mindful of what unclean state this man was in that he didn't want to get messy, dirty, or unclean himself. Perhaps he looked down at him with contempt. The priest did not offer to pray for him. He did not offer to intercede for him. He did not act as a mediator between him and God. He did not want to get his hands dirty because he was too clean. I wonder if he prayed for the injured man as he walked by. Or, perhaps the priest failed to get into God's presence that day. He failed to start his day seeking God's will and direction and didn't hear God's still, small voice. He wasn't carrying God's heart with him. If he had, how would it have impacted his perspective?

We likely have had the attitude of this priest at some point in our lives. Maybe the priest could not identify with the man's situation. When we cannot identify with another, we tend to judge the person rather than the injustice they are experiencing. Priests were good at judgment. Lepers had to submit to priests for purification to determine their cleanliness. It would have been easy for the priest to judge the injured man: *He must be a troublemaker. He was doing something illegal. It was his fault.* Perhaps he felt the man deserved what he got: *If he hadn't put himself in such a position—in the wrong place, at the wrong hour, or hanging with the wrong crowd—maybe that would not have happened to him.* Do those questions sound familiar? They reek of judgment, not compassion.

In the book of Job, when Job experiences affliction, his friends judge him instead of helping him. Were they justified in their judgment? No, they were not. They were scorned by God for judging another man's afflictions. Jesus said in Matthew 7:1-2, "Judge not, that you be not judged. For with what judgement you judge, you will be judged; and with the measure you use, it will be measured back to you." We all have a judgment day ahead of us. I want the measure of grace, not judgment, used for me. How about you?

Perhaps the priest was more concerned with looking good than doing good. Maybe he was more concerned about doing good at the temple than outside the temple. Are you doing good things in your church but ignoring everyone outside your church? Do you separate your "secular" life from your "spiritual" life? This is the same attitude that tempts us to say, "Look at me! I sing on the worship team. I serve as an elder and give marriage counsel. I usher in the tithes and offering. I lead the children." But what about in the *real* world, outside the church doors? What do you do where it matters more in your community, especially for those who never walk inside your church?

The priest represented the church, religious and spiritual maturity, but he did not speak up. Sometimes it's easier to send money to a missionary in another country than to love other cultures in your own backyard; but what happens to a neighborhood, community, and nation when the spiritually mature do not speak up or act? What is happening in your world today that you are ignoring?

We question what is happening in our nation today, but are the spiritually mature speaking up?

## THE LEVITE

Likewise a Levite, when he arrived at the place, came and looked, and passed by on the other side.

Luke 10:32

Levites, who were also descendants of Aaron, served as assistants to the priests. They performed menial duties outlined in the book of Numbers, taking care of the tabernacle and temple. During most of the year, they lived in their own cities, but at fixed periods they worked at the tabernacle. They did good work because they did God's work: preparing the place of worship. Yet, the Levite in the parable missed the purpose of God's work in this situation. What good is preparing God's house for worship if you are not truly willing to serve His people? Instead, the Levite followed the same heart response as his leader, the priest.

How many of us follow in the footsteps of our leaders, parents, or grandparents even when it is not right? Were they ignorant, lacking compassion, unforgiving, or prejudiced? Did we speak out or did we walk in their same footsteps? Maybe we don't voice it, but deep in our hearts we are no different. Committing an offense and staying silent about an offense are the same thing. Many of us—most of us—need to truly dig deep and examine the hatred, ignorance, and prejudices that were taught or passed on to us. Maybe you don't act on prejudice, but have you done anything to remove it from your core belief system or your heart's response?

Who have you judged, avoided, or not helped because of what you have been taught about that race, culture, religion, or status? Who have you looked at in the face of their transgression and walked away from because it was not your problem? The Levite might have been thinking about helping the wounded man, but he had too many tasks waiting for him back at the temple. He was more concerned with the task than what the task was meant to accomplish: healing people.

So many times in life we are just too busy. We are too busy with menial tasks that make us miss the big picture. We miss our kids' childhoods, family celebrations, and our spouse's feelings—all of the things that are immediately surrounding us. We are, therefore, much more easily distracted from those who are hurting from afar, down the street, across the tracks, or over the wall. What tasks are keeping you from noticing the injustices around you? Don't allow the tasks you have been gifted with become bigger than who the gifts are for.

The priest and Levite are examples of moments in our own lives when we don't reach out to people, especially those outside our purview. People of faith, for example, often get caught up in their own faith-based world: going to church, going to Bible study, going to small groups, eating, fellowshipping, and working with those who believe as they do. Christians forget about or ignore the nonbeliever, casting judgment like Job's friends. Have you ever looked at someone and thought, *If they followed Jesus, they wouldn't be in the mess they are in*? Is this also our attitude toward race?

It was the job of the priest and the Levite to help, but they chose to ignore the hurting man. Something else was more important. A friend of mine told me that many times in education, intellect is used more than the heart. She shared that when a student fits a certain statistic from a particular culture or socioeconomic status, or has a high transient rate, it's easy to presume that student will not perform well. *That student will be distracted. Loud. Obnoxious. Misbehaved.* Teachers may cringe at the thought of having *that* student in the classroom with thirty other kids. Even though it is the teacher's job to help that student, it can be easier to ignore him or her and the issues. The priest and the Levite also likely felt it would be easier to ignore the troubled man and his issues.

This may ring a bell for many of you more than the previous points. It does for me. Let's assume the Levite avoided the injustice because, frankly, he didn't know what to do. He just couldn't handle the pain. He could handle good news because he was used to working at the temple where his work brings glory to God, where the harps play worship music and the angels sing. He could not, however, handle the sad, horrific, tragic news. Or maybe he would care too much and become angry. Maybe he would have unforgiveness toward the offenders. Is this starting to sound familiar? What if the Levite or the priest were offended by what the injured man represented and the reason they ignored him was because they could not emotionally deal with the pain? Maybe it reminded them of the bondage and slavery in Egypt.

If we put it into context, how many times do we convince ourselves that we can't do anything, because? Because we don't know what to do. Because if we act, we would have hatred toward the government, the White House, the church, the Democrats, the Republicans, the Canadians, the French, the police, the conservatives, the liberals, the whites, the illegals, the blacks, the Muslims. How many of us ignore bad news, traumatic events, or extremely sad situations for the very same reason? We tell ourselves that we "just can't handle it." The world is too messy, too traumatic, too political; there is too much injustice.

The truth is, that news brief we ignored represents a real life, real people, real pain. It is actually a good sign that we turn off the ugly news we hear; it shows we mourn the evil in this world. The situation we can't tolerate hearing about, however, is 100 percent real for those involved. People cannot be set free, healed, or liberated if we—those who are free, healed, and liberated—avoid their troubles.

I have a friend whose child suffered from a rare disease, and I realized that I did not pray for her as I should have, nor did I handle her catastrophic challenges appropriately. Because of my lack of experience and knowledge about what to do, I found it too difficult to think about. I was looking at the situation from my own perspective rather than from God's perspective.

I have another friend who, for years, has been very passionate about social justice and I neglected to get involved in her conversations because I could not handle them. I actually cared deeply about the same things. I just couldn't allow my heart to open to the pain I saw and felt about the subject. I pushed my concern deep within, knowing that if I chose to expose it, it would only turn into hatred and anger toward those involved. I chose to ignore it.

While I was at the Holocaust museum in Jerusalem, I read this quote by Imre Bathory, who served in the Righteous Among the Nations organization in Hungary, and it resonated in my heart.: "I know that when I stand before God on judgment day I shall not be asked the question posed to Cane—where were you when your brother's blood was crying out to God?"

If we have God's perspective on how to handle sad, traumatic, and even evil news, He will give us the wisdom, discernment, and strength to walk through any situation. I've learned from experience that ignoring and turning away is not a solution or an option. Jesus never sat back and did nothing. Instead of walking away like the Levite, ask yourself what God's perspective is on the issues of injustice, hatred, division, and assaults against humanity. What is His solution? What would His response be?

## THE SAMARITAN

But a certain Samaritan, as he journeyed, came where he was. And when he saw him, he had compassion.

Luke 10:33

This sentence is earth-shaking. Life-changing. Bridge-making. The Samaritan—the historically oppressed, discriminated, excluded, downcast, and rebuked race in Jerusalem—does something miraculous. He shows compassion to a man of a different race, a race that contributed to the social injustice he and his people have endured for hundreds of years. It's very possible the injured man himself contributed to the discrimination, the pain, and the hurt of the Samaritan people.

The Samaritan man, I'm sure, was very aware of his surroundings and that most other travelers on the road were Jews. The hatred between Jews and Samaritans was at its height when Jesus shared this parable. At one point, the Pharisees even called Jesus a "Samaritan devil" (John 8:48 NLT) while in a debate with Him. It was not a good time in history. Women, children, and people of other races were not treated equally. Though hard to imagine, the climate was darker even than the hatred, discrimination, and social injustice we experience today. Women and children could easily be killed, abused, or beaten for any reason—or no reason at all.

I have no doubt that some of you reading this can identify with this reality. It brings real pain and real experiences to life. That is why the Samaritan's actions make this story even more eye-opening. The Samaritan could have allowed the abuse, depreciation, and dismissal of his people to harden his heart. He could have responded from offense. Instead, he approached the beaten, broken-down Jew, and responded with compassion.

He could have taken what was left of the man's dignity. He could have kicked him while he was down. He could have excused his actions based on the oppression his people had endured for generations. Neither his family, friends, nor his community would have blamed him. They might have even praised him. He could have rejoiced that the Jewish man got what was coming to him, that the Jew could finally see *what it feels like.*

Instead, the Samaritan had compassion. He could relate to the pain, the shame, the harassment. If we let them, our troubles can make us more compassionate toward others in trouble.

> So he went to him and bandaged his wounds, pouring on oil and wine; and he set him on his own animal, brought him to an inn, and took care of him. On the next day, when he departed, he took out two denarii, gave them to the innkeeper, and said to him, "Take care of him; and whatever more you spend, when I come again, I will repay you."
>
> Luke 10:34-35

At that time in history, a priest was highly regarded—a Samaritan was not. A Levite had access to the high priest—a Samaritan did not. The Samaritan did not have access to the religious elite or the temple in Jerusalem, yet he was more Christ-like than all of the others. The Samaritan dug deep, to a place in his heart that remembered the pain of having his identity stripped, stolen, ignored, and ruined. He and the injured Jew had something in common: they both had been wounded and oppressed; they both knew injustice.

Maybe you know what it is like to be judged for the color of your skin. You have been looked down upon because of your age. You have been denied influence because of your gender. You have been presumed less capable because of your race. You have been profiled when you were, in fact, innocent. And worse, you have seen others who look like you unjustly wounded to the point of death. There is a real enemy that comes to kill, steal, and destroy.

What would you do if you were in the same situation as the Samaritan? Would you respond with anger, or mercy? Would you walk in forgiveness, or stir up retaliation, hatred, and offense?

The Samaritan chose to carry the man's burden, at least for a short time. In the midst of this, he did not complain about "the man," or "the system," and how unfair life was. He did not encourage bitterness. He did not feed hatred. He did not take on a victim mentality. He did not fight in the name of social justice that takes on the form of hatred, pride, and retaliation. He did not leave the injured man the way he was but helped restore him in the way he deserved.

The Samaritan chose the path of reconciliation, the path that Jesus demonstrated to us over and over again. Which path will we choose?

# CHAPTER 5

# THE CHALLENGE

Peace to you. Just as the Father
sent me, I send you.

JOHN 20:21 MSG

In the parable of the good Samaritan, Jesus expressed the true character of a neighbor through the different actions of the priest, the Levite, and the Samaritan. He unveiled the motives—good and bad—that we each carry in our hearts toward one another and showed us what they look like when lived out. Jesus used this long parable just to answer one question—who our neighbor is—in order to reveal *His* heart and solution: mercy. "So which of these three do you think was neighbor to him who fell among the thieves?" (Luke 10:36).

Your neighbor is anyone, of any race, gender, or social status, who needs your help. Your neighbor is someone who may have hurt you, offended you, and oppressed you—or your ancestors. Your neighbor is someone who has nothing in common with you on the surface but who shares the one thing we all have in common: we are children of the Creator of heaven and Earth.

We are all neighbors. The only way to see ourselves as neighbors is to focus on what unites us, not what divides us. If you recall, the lawyer in the parable originally questioned Jesus not out of curiosity or sincerity, but to catch Jesus in a trap and allow division in his heart. At the end of the parable, Jesus asked him directly which character was neighbor to the injured man. After examining each person's response, finally the lawyer answered Jesus, "He who showed mercy on him" (Luke 10:37).

In the lawyer's initial interaction with Jesus, he quotes the law from Deuteronomy and Leviticus, but he leaves out part of Leviticus 19:18: "You shall not take vengeance, nor bear any grudge against the children of your people." When he answered Jesus at the end of the parable, he refused to actually say the word "Samaritan," the name of the people who happened to be children of his ancestors.

Sadly, his heart had not truly changed. Some of us may find ourselves ignoring or intentionally leaving out God's Word or principals to cover our own prejudices, judgment, and pride. What kind of neighbor are *you*? Do you need to expand the definition of "neighbors" in your life? It was difficult for the lawyer to say the name "Samaritan," or admit he was a "good neighbor," considering how Samaritans were socially treated at the time. The lawyer was still not willing to see or admit to the problem that was at hand.

Are you willing to open your heart to determine where you have been blind? Or, like the lawyer, are you still in a place where you are unwilling to admit there are people in your world who need to be seen, who need compassion, who need your help and your voice? Can you relate, perhaps, to the innkeeper? He was not likely trying to contribute to the harmful situation; but he did not go out of his way to help. He ran his business the way he always had. He provided a service in exchange for payment. He was willing to benefit from the situation financially. There is nothing necessarily morally wrong with that. He just did not contribute to the healing or reconciling of the situation. He simply accepted a customer for a fee. He may have said to himself, *Well, I did not hurt him. I did not contribute to his pain. It was not my father or grandfather who oppressed his people. I did not enslave him. My grandfather was not a slave owner. Don't look at me. It's not my fault.* How many of us feel it's not our concern to help heal a broken person or situation simply because we did not directly cause it? Do we proclaim God's love for others but refuse to show that love with our own actions, like the innkeeper, lawyer, priest, or Levite? The truth is, we may be indirectly contributing to the issue simply by our lack of willingness to do something about it. We're contributing to the pain by remaining quiet. Not speaking up. Not seeking to understand what issues are at hand. Not seeking how to reconcile the issue. But instead, just going on with our own daily life, minding our own business. Is that what it means to be a neighbor?

## THE QUESTION

The first question the lawyer asks at the beginning of the parable is how to inherit the Kingdom of God. Jesus' answer was simple: love God and love others. The second question is to qualify who the "others" are who we need to love. The antagonistic question of the lawyer reveals a hard, non-empathetic heart that is also reflected by the thieves, priest, Levite, and even the innkeeper. But truly, it reflects back to us our own non-compassionate hearts toward other races, religions, and cultures. The answer to the second question, of course, is "everyone." We need to love everyone, including those who ignore us, discriminate against us, retaliate, take advantage of our situations, and even those who want to use our situations as a political platform or social debate.

We show love by providing mercy. I once read "mercy" described as withholding something that is owed, whereas grace is giving something that is not owed. Mercy is withholding judgment when it is deserved. Grace is giving love when it is not deserved. In the parable, we are taught to provide mercy to our neighbor, our community, on social media posts, through political agendas, and in religious debates. Perhaps compassion is having a balance of both mercy and grace. Jesus showed us it is impossible to truly love God with all our hearts if we do not also love His people with all of our hearts. That is His requirement.

In a recent message I heard from Chris Hodges, senior pastor and founder of Church of the Highlands in Alabama, he told a dramatic story of when he lost his autistic son for a short time—that seemed like eternity. Those of us who have misplaced a child for some time can identify. He went through the dramatic and scary details of what he imagined happened to his child. He shared how intense he was about finding *this one* son, knowing that the other four children were safe. But he valued his son so much, he needed to find the one who was missing. He shared, "When something has value to me, and it is missing, gone wrong, hurt, in pain . . . I do something about it!"

As he shared those words, it hit me. Here is the problem: people don't have value to us! If people of other cultures, social backgrounds, and races had value to us, what would we do differently? When you love God, you can't help but love the people whom Jesus loves. It is not about what I like and what makes me comfortable; it's about Him. Who and what does Jesus love?

Chris also shared John 4:35, where Jesus told the disciples to lift up their eyes to see what He sees. The Message version reads: "Well, I am telling you to open your eyes and take a good look at what's right in front of you. These Samaritan fields are ripe. It's harvest time!" Chris reminded us that Jesus told His disciples to open their eyes because they were not looking at the world with their spiritual eyes but only with their natural eyes. They were seeing the world through their lenses of prejudice, traditions, religion, but not through the lens of God's heart. Some people have natural vision issues and are diagnosed as nearsighted, meaning they can see well near them but things that are far away are unfocused or blurry. The problem with the Levite and the priest in the parable is that their vision was "nearsighted." They were not focused on things that did not concern them but were selfishly focused on things within or near them.

In other words, we don't feel responsible for what we don't see. If we aren't willing to open our eyes to see, we may miss what is going on around us. We often focus only on ourselves or what immediately affects our family, but what about our neighbors, community, city, state, country, and world? Are you nearsighted with other people's issues because you deem they have nothing to do with you? Are you walking around them or across the street to avoid them because you do not share the same experiences, issues, pains, or obstacles?

It's easy to get away from what is really going on around us if we only focus on ourselves. When we look up, we can actually *see* what needs to be done. We need to be *farsighted* as well as nearsighted. The Levite and the priest intentionally walked across the street to avoid the hurting man. If you love God, if you love Jesus, then you love who He loves and you care for their issues. Open up your eyes to see what is happening around you!

## THE ANSWER

I love this part. Right at the end of the parable of the good Samaritan, Jesus gives a command—a solution—to the lawyer: "Then Jesus said to him, 'Go and do likewise'" (Luke 10:37).

Jesus says to go and do. Both of those words are verbs. We called them action words in my elementary school. Go! Do! It is clear that in order to make a difference in this world, to truly show your love, action is required. James 2 reminds us of this very principle:

> You see that a person is considered righteous by what they do and not by faith alone. In the same way, was not even Rahab the prostitute considered righteous for what she did when she gave lodging to the spies and sent them off in a different direction? As the body without the spirit is dead, so faith without deeds is dead.
>
> James 2:24-26 NIV

You can do nothing or you can do something. Either one reveals your true faith. What did each character *do* in the parable? The lawyer discussed. The thieves exploited. The religious men ignored and avoided. The innkeeper served for a fee. The Samaritan *went* and *served*. Go. Do.

Who are *you* in this parable? Who do you want to be going forward? Unlike the woman at the well, who Jesus went out of His way to go see, the hurt man was lying in their direct path. Who is lying in your path? Do you step out of the way and ignore them? Not only do we have to do something in order to show our love, but also many times we need to go out of our way, just like Jesus did. Sometimes we do not want to get involved in the drama of another person's mess. Thank God Jesus did. In the book of Mark, when Jesus ministers to the lepers, we see that Jesus was willing to risk being unclean, as lepers were considered, in order to make someone else clean. James reminds us that taking action is an important part of having faith:

> What *does it* profit, my brethren, if someone says he has faith but does not have works? Can faith save him? If a brother or sister is naked and destitute of daily food, and one of you says to them, "Depart in peace, be warmed and filled," but you do not give them the things which are needed for the body, what *does it* profit? Thus also faith by itself, if it does not have works, is dead.
>
> James 2:14-17

Are you willing to get dirty to do the work of Jesus Christ? To *where* or *what* is God calling you to *go*, and to *where* or *what* is He calling you to *do*? One of the last things Jesus said to His disciples before ascending to heaven is reported in Matthew 28:18-20, also known as the Great Commission:

> And Jesus came and spoke to them, saying, "All authority has been given to Me in heaven and on earth. Go therefore and make disciples of all the nations, baptizing them in the name of the Father and of the Son and of the Holy Spirit, teaching them to observe all things that I have commanded you."

This is a command from Jesus—not an option—to go and love all people. Jesus chose to share the parable of the good Samaritan with us to remind us that unconditional love is deliberate, intentional, and out of our comfort zone. The salvation and reconciliation of lives does not happen without you and me.

# CHAPTER 6

# RENEWED UNITY

> If someone has enough money to live well and sees a brother or sister in need but shows no compassion—how can God's love be in that person? Dear children, let's not merely say that we love each other; let us show the truth by our actions.
>
> 1 JOHN 3:17-18

After the crucifixion and resurrection, Jesus' earthly ministry was complete, at least until His return. He shared hope and healing, and He destroyed the tomb. He passed the baton to His disciples—you and me—to spread His ministry to the entire world. To reconcile. To love. To serve. The book of Acts picks up from the last chapters of Matthew, Mark, and Luke where Jesus shared the great commission. In His very last words, Samaria is *specifically* named before He ascends to heaven: "But you shall receive power when the Holy Spirit has come upon you; and you shall be witnesses to Me in Jerusalem, and in all Judea and Samaria, and to the end of the earth" (Acts 1:8).

Samaria. A historical place of division, oppression, rejection, racial tension, and social injustice is specifically named by the King of kings, the Lord of Hosts, the Shepherd, the Word, the Alpha and Omega, the Resurrection. The Savior tore the veil, taking with it all pride, all prejudice, all bondage. He set the captives free. The Samaritan half breed that had been under the chains of prejudice for 750 years was not only set free but also received an invitation from the Messiah Himself to partake in the spreading of the good news. He ordained His disciples, whom He personally trained and mentored during His three-year ministry, to specifically take steps into Samaria and replicate His work.

Though the disciples saw Jesus speak to the woman at the well, remembered being rebuked for suggesting killing the Samaritans in a village, and heard the parable of the good Samaritan, they had not completely understood the revelation of Jesus' ministry: to extend into *all* the world. The Gospel was not only for the Jew, Jesus' race, but also for every race and *mixed race* in Samaria and in the uttermost parts of the world. The love of Jesus extends to every race, gender, and social class yesterday, today, and tomorrow.

Had Jesus not specifically named Samaria, the followers of Christ may not have shared the Gospel outside of their communities. Persecution of the followers of Christ, led by Saul, forced the disciples out of Jerusalem and into Samaria and Judea. Philip, one of the chosen seven men to help distribute food among widows and the poor in the church, was obedient in following Jesus' words. He was one of the first to preach the Gospel outside of Jerusalem, going into Samaria and preaching to those in refuge and those who needed to hear the Gospel.

> At that time a great persecution arose against the church which was at Jerusalem; and they were all scattered throughout the regions of Judea and Samaria, except the apostles.

And devout men carried Stephen to his burial and made great lamentation over him. As for Saul, he made havoc of the church, entering every house, and dragging off men and women, committing them to prison.

Therefore those who were scattered went everywhere preaching the word. Then Philip went down to the city of Samaria and preached Christ to them. And the multitudes with one accord heeded the things spoken by Philip, hearing and seeing the miracles which he did. For unclean spirits, crying with a loud voice, came out of many who were possessed; and many who were paralyzed and lame were healed. And there was great joy in that city.

Acts 8:1-8

Let's not read over this too quickly. Despite racial hatred, Jesus went to Samaria. He extended reconciliation to a woman and her people. He used a parable to illustrate reconciliation and then ordained His disciples to go and do the same. Philip was obedient and, because of that, there was great healing and rejoicing in the city and among the people. Philip *went*; Samaritans *heard* the Gospel, *saw* the testimonies, received *healing*, and experienced *joy*. Jesus desires the good news to be shared and experienced through, to, and by all people.

Are you willing to be bold and courageous to communicate and collaborate with people you historically have not had a good relationship with? Will you be bold enough to be one of the first to do this in your family? In your community? In your church? Philip did not limit himself to a particular people group; he *went* where most would not go because of an age-old accepted prejudice. He did what Jesus did, even in the midst of the most difficult time and under spiritual and physical persecution.

There is never a convenient time to do God's work. In fact, if it is convenient and easy it may not be God at all. The power of God's love witnessed to the disciples, and they eventually learned that the unaccepted were meant to be accepted. In Acts 8:14-17, 25, John and Peter go to Samaria as well. This is incredible. This is the critical follow-through that sealed the work of the Holy Spirit in the Samaritans' lives.

> Now when the apostles who were at Jerusalem heard that Samaria had received the word of God, they sent Peter and John to them, who, when they had come down, prayed for them that they might receive the Holy Spirit. For as yet He had fallen upon none of them. They had only been baptized in the name of the Lord Jesus. Then they laid hands on them, and they received the Holy Spirit. . . . So when they had testified and preached the word of the Lord, they returned to Jerusalem, preaching the gospel in many villages of the Samaritans.

What a powerful moment. The Gospel *and* the Holy Spirit touched Samaria. The place of hatred, division, prejudice, judgment, offense became a place of healing, unity, and power! John and Peter went to provide unity among the brethren because they were no longer divided. They were spiritually connected and unified. The power of God would finally grow and prosper the church because of the unity in Christ Jesus between the once feuding races. We have the same ability today to unite our community and nation. "Then the churches throughout Judea, Galilee, and Samaria had peace and were edified. And walking in the fear of the Lord and in the comfort of the Holy Spirit, they were multiplied" (Act 9:31).

There had not been that kind of peace in Samaria since King Solomon reigned over all of Israel and Judah. See what happens when there is unity in the land and among the people? The formation of the Samaritan people came from an attempt to tear apart, but Christ came to bring unity in places where even kings, people, and the world intended to cause division. Jesus is the Prince of Peace and allows us to have peace with our Father first, in our hearts second, and then with each other.

Three amazing things happened in order for unity to take place between the Jews and the Samaritans. First, the people of Samaria *opened* their eyes to the unifying Gospel of Jesus. They accepted it! They did not hold a grudge. They did not reject the Gospel of the Jews but laid down their own defenses and offenses and humbly accepted the good news, opening the door to God's power in their lives. In what area in your life have you felt rejected, offended, or hurt and need to lay down your pride? Jesus says to ask and you shall receive (see Matthew 7:7). However, some of us have our hands and eyes closed, and we are not willing to truly accept the gifts God has for us. Are you ready to receive wholeness, healing, and truth? Jesus wants to give you beauty for ashes (see Isaiah 61).

Second, the Jews, those who previously judged the Samaritans, went to Samaria. John was the one who asked Jesus if they should pray for fire from heaven to burn down on a Samaritan village in Luke 9:51-55. Then, John and Peter laid down their own experiences of rejection and hatred to fully embrace, love, and bring healing to the Samaritans so that the church could accomplish its mission to unify God's people: all the people in the world. Jesus prayed for this very thing right before He was betrayed and crucified. He prayed for the completion of His assignment, He prayed for His disciples, and then He prayed for you and me.

I do not pray for these alone, but also for those who will believe in Me through their word; that they all may be one, as You, Father, are in Me, and I in You; that they also may be one in Us, that the world may believe that You sent Me. And the glory which You gave Me I have given them, that they may be one just as We are one: I in them, and You in Me; that they may be made perfect in one, and that the world may know that You have sent Me, and have loved them as You have loved Me.

John 17:20-23

Just as He was—and is—unified with God the Father, Jesus prayed that we too would be unified with Him and with each other. How important this prayer is! How intentional. Jesus was preparing to be taken to Jerusalem for His trial. His work was done. Then He stopped to pray for us, them, the world. In that same passage, Jesus said that He gave us the power, the same power God gave Him—to be made perfect in one—so that the world would know that God sent Jesus to Earth and that He loves them.

Brothers and sisters, it is our job to go and do so that we can be unified with our heavenly Father, so that we are witnesses to the world of God's love. The world is completely divided, lost, and confused. However, how can we help heal the world if our church is also divided racially, socially, or politically? God's people cannot be divided. A divided house cannot stand (see Mark 3:25). God made us to be different from the feuding world. There is beauty in diversity, unlike division. Our differences are meant to complement one another, just as our different gifts are meant to come together as parts of a body, to make up one body with one purpose: to build and glorify His Church.

John and Peter were very different in temperament. In the book of John, John describes himself as the beloved. He was in tune with his emotions, but Peter was zealous, ready to cut off ears in the name of justice. John took pleasure in his Father's love, while Peter risked his life to jump off a boat and attempt to walk on water. They were different, but they had one goal: unity.

First Corinthians 12:12-14, 26 describes unity:

For as the body is one and has many members, but all the members of that one body, being many, are one body, so also is Christ. For by one Spirit we were all baptized into one body—whether Jews or Greeks, whether slaves or free—and have all been made to drink into one Spirit. For in fact the body is not one member but many. . . . And if one member suffers, all the members suffer with it; or if one member is honored, all the members rejoice with it.

While John and Peter were complete opposites, they traveled together, worked together, and ministered to the people together, bringing the power of the Holy Spirit into Samaria. The powerful and dramatic filling of the Holy Spirit in Samaria signifies a special moment in history when God's people united, despite their differences. This happened again when Cornelius, a Gentile, and his family received the Holy Spirit. God is for all people. It was a critical moment in history: the unifying of races bound by a racial divide hundreds of years old.

The third, and final, thing that took place in order for unity to prevail was when Saul encountered Jesus and became the apostle Paul. Saul, prior to his conversion, persecuted, killed, and imprisoned many Christians. Many times, we see Jesus as the savior of the downtrodden, the underdog, the outcast. We don't always see Him as the savior of the tyrant. Nor do we want to. And that may be the very thing keeping us from reconciling with the hearts and minds of others.

We are not always willing to pray for the abuser, the murderer, the pimp, the corrupt officer, and the slave owner, even though Jesus tells us to pray for our enemies (see Matthew 5:44). Are you willing to go, do, and pray for someone who is opposed to you, your life, your religion, your race, or your gender for the advancement and unity of His Church? What power, freedom, and salvation of souls may be waiting for you to do so? What can happen when a Nebuchadnezzar or Saul of Tarsus or the President of the United States is reconciled and saved by Jesus Christ? Look at how much greater the glory and testimony of God are revealed when someone leaves the darkness to live a life in the light.

Ironically, the church became marked by the same experience that the Samaritan people walked in for centuries. It was birthed during a horrific time of persecution and of people fleeing to save their lives. They were then rejected for generations due to hatred and division. Philip fled Jerusalem after Stephen was martyred. His life was on the line. There was a death sentence out for those preaching the Gospel. It was not a time of peace and prosperity. In the midst of an extremely dangerous time, people were willing to unconditionally love and accept one another, lay down their generational differences, and unite for *one cause*. That cause gave them power, encouragement, and hope that would last a lifetime.

Today, there is so much division among different people groups in America and across the globe. There are school shootings, suicides, political unrest, trafficking of women and children, and uprisings of racial divide. The trepidation is great. The time is ripe once again. We can spread the love now more than ever. There is immense persecution happening today—of women, of children, of religions, of races, of identity. The list goes on. It is time to unite the people of this earth and the people of God like never before. It is possible now like it was during the time of Christ. We have to be willing to go, to be proactive and initiate reconciliation.

As a Christian, one who has been reconciled to God through Jesus Christ, you now have the ministry of reconciliation, the duty to help reconcile others to Christ. It is your role to go and do something for those who are divided, lost, or excluded. It is your role to share with them the good news and reveal the miraculous works of God in their lives that will lead to healing, freedom, and the ultimate joy. Does Jesus limit what we are responsible to help reconcile as Christians? Are you a reconciler for those dealing with racial injustice, gender inequality, and social divide? It may be easy to imagine yourself as a reconciler for someone with an addiction, abuse, or anger problem. The truth is, any transgression holding us back from the complete restoration in God needs reconciling.

## THE POWER OF A UNIFIED CHURCH

The Church continued to expand among the Jews, Samaritans, and those who believed in God. Then, in Acts 10, Peter had a revelation that Gentiles could receive salvation too. Peter had a vision in which God spoke to him, opening the door for a Gentile family to receive Jesus. This experience eventually served as an invitation for all Gentiles to receive the Gospel. This was the greatest news for all of the non-Hebrew world.

Up to that point, the followers of Jesus were all Jewish believers. They were unified according to Acts 9:31, per Jesus' prayer and directions carried out in Acts 1:8 and 8:14-15. They destroyed division and unified the Christian church from Jerusalem to Samaria and Galilee. Once the Jewish believers were unified, they were finally able to spread the Gospel to the non-Jewish world, even those who did not know or have a relationship with God. They unified, and then they reached out to those lost in a dark world, with no hope, no light, no direction, and no salvation. The influence of the united Christian church was finally spreading to nonbelievers. Do you see the connection? The pattern? The same is true for us today.

> Then he said to them, "You know how unlawful it is for a Jewish man to keep company with or go to one of another nation. But God has shown me that I should not call any man common or unclean. . . . Then Peter opened his mouth and said: "In truth I perceive that God shows no partiality. But in every nation whoever fears Him and works righteousness is accepted by Him. . . . And those of the circumcision who believed were astonished, as many as came with Peter, because the gift of the Holy Spirit had been poured out on the Gentiles also.
>
> Acts 10:28, 34-35, 45

Acts 11 tells us how Christianity was launched in Antioch of Syria to the Gentiles, even though it was the center for heathen cults that celebrated sexual immorality and other evil practices. Our world is full of sexual promiscuity, pornography, and exploitation, even in the cities we call home. The world, our country, and our communities need the Gospel. The Church, followers of Jesus Christ, must be united so that we can teach the unbelieving world. We cannot be divided in our hearts, nor can we be divided racially, financially, socially, or politically, otherwise we are unable to show the world the solution to the things that divide us. Let's show the world, once more, that we are united in Christ, not divided by race, culture, or class.

It is easy to get distracted and focus on the wrong thing. It is easy to fight and argue over different theologies within the church, instruments and dancing on the worship team, titles within church leadership, which songs should be sung. It can be difficult to wrestle with political parties and polarized social issues at hand. It is painful and frustrating to witness the horrible tragedies on the news: murder, rape, manipulation. It is a trap to get offended by our very own sisters, parents, pastors, or even the leader of our nation. When we do not remember our position on the "team," it is easy to get distracted.

I had an opportunity to meet the first female NFL coach, Dr. Jen Welter, at a conference. She said her number-one goal was to simply distract the offensive player. Even though the running back, wide receiver, or tight end has a very specific job, and a very specific play with very specific footsteps, he can get distracted. All the offensive player has to do is run left or right or back or slanted, just how he practiced all week, watched in film, read in the playbook, and even discussed in the huddle, but he can easily be distracted by the defensive player, who would simply have to follow him, whisper to him, taunt him, and insult him. That is the main goal of the defender: make the offensive player misstep by distracting him. They can impact the offensive players by their demeanor before the ball is even snapped. We've seen it a dozen times. A quarterback throws a very specific pass to the very talented and high-paid receiver who is completely distracted, overwhelmed, and off track because of the defender.

This is the position the Church is in, and also for any Christian who has allowed the voices, offenses, media, racism, and the world's division to distract them from the goal of winning. We are here to win more than a game, but the lives of lost souls. We cannot win if we're distracted from walking in unity, and maybe more importantly, the *reason* for unity. In his book *Influence*, Mike Hayes writes, "What a force of influence in the world we could be if we all possessed the splendor of perfect unity" (p. 80).

In Genesis 11, we read the story of the Tower of Babel. We know that mankind, at that time, spoke one language and sought to make itself great in its own eyes by building a tall monument to honor man, known as the Tower of Babel. The people were in great unity that created such power that God Himself said in Genesis 11:6, "Indeed the people *are* one and they all have one language, and this is what they begin to do; now nothing that they propose to do will be withheld from them." This is the power of unity. Nothing is impossible when we walk in unity with our brethren. Unfortunately for those people, they were unified in selfish and prideful motives, removing God from their agenda. The monument was not for God's glory and work in the earth but for their own. In order to eliminate the tower, God caused confusion by giving them different languages.

If we are not careful, we too can become unified in a worldly agenda that builds a political, social, racial, or religious tower of our own design rather than God's. God wants us to be unified but rooted in Him. You and I have to set down any monument that we have allowed to overshadow God's agenda in our lives, and that includes our gender, our race, our social status, or our financial status. We are not great because of these statues in our lives. They simply separate us from God in our prideful hearts.

Have you ever listened to a beautiful melody sung by a performer, only to be shocked by their actual native speaking voice? I have listened to actresses and musical artists from Great Britain or Australia sing in perfect harmony with someone from America, or another country, and while they have different speaking accents, they can choose to harmonize to the same sound when singing.

In the story of the Tower of Babel, the people were divided by their different languages, but God had a plan to bring them back into perfect harmony. In the very next chapter, He blessed Abraham, and through Abraham's lineage came the Savior. Jesus then walked the earth and told His disciples that the Helper would come. In Acts 2:1-11, the outpouring of the Holy Spirit came so that, though the people spoke in different tongues, they understood each other. The barrier that had separated the people by gender, race, and socioeconomic status, and even language, was finally removed. They were one in perfect harmony, unified through the power of the Holy Spirit.

Centuries later, in America, black slaves and white abolitionists prayed and worshiped together in unity, eventually achieving victory through the abolishment of slavery. Unity is what brought about the end of segregation. Change and reconciliation are only possible when we choose unity. It is time for the Church to reunite once again. We have the power to speak the same tongue and language of our Lord and Savior and to lead our nation and this world away from dividing issues and into renewed unity in Christ.

# CHAPTER 7

# EXAMINE THE HEART

I will give you a new heart and put a new spirit within you; I will take the heart of stone out of your flesh and give you a heart of flesh.

EZEKIEL 36:26

Our assignment is clear: love our neighbors and bring reconciliation and unity to our divided world. It sounds simple, straightforward, but how do we accomplish the task? It begins with an examination of our hearts. We need to truly examine our hearts to determine where we are, who we are, and what we believe so that we can bring reconciliation out of a pure heart. If we are to love our neighbors, it cannot be simply out of obligation—though we should honor obligations; it should come sincerely out of the love of Christ to be effective. Love has deeper roots than obligation. The lawyer who spoke to Jesus in the parable of the good Samaritan had an opportunity to examine his heart, but he chose to walk in prejudice even after Jesus showed him the answer to the Kingdom of God: forgiveness, compassion, and love for another race of people. The good news is that God is a forgiving God of repenting hearts.

## FORGIVENESS

Years ago, I had a friend whom I loved very much. She was creative, beautiful, and a joy to be around. We spent years together in our circle of friends within our church in different ministries. Our church, like many, went through a transition and she and her husband decided to leave. Some time passed and I did not hear from her, and I became genuinely concerned about her, so I called her. I texted her. No response. Weeks went by with nothing in return and it started to concern me. The more I texted and called her with no response, the more upset I got. I, too, was still hurting from the church transition and did not understand the silence. She was my friend. I could confide in her and she could confide in me. We had done so for years. I was finally fed up and convinced it was my job to tell her how bad of a friend she was by not even giving me the courtesy of a response.

That said, you actually need a person to answer their phone in order to give them a piece of your mind. After a few months, I got a response from her saying she was not in a good place and was trying to process life and even friendships. I had compassion and told her I understood and would give her room to process. I got it. She needed time to heal. More time went by and I still heard nothing from her. I would send her short texts now and then just to let her know I was praying for her. She would send a short response, but nothing of substance. What made things worse is that I heard from several friends that she was still communicating with them and even going out of her way to go to dinner with them. I was confused, hurt, and outright angry.

I sent a text one day and asked if she was ready to have friends again. Her response caught me completely off guard. She wrote, "What do you really want from me?" In my mind, she was questioning my motives, as if I had ill intention. I was livid. She did not even have the decency to pick up the phone and explain to me what was going on. I had to communicate through limited text. This was before data would allow you to send novels via text like today. I wanted to tell her off, but I knew that would just shut her down and not give me a chance to know what was going on.

That is what I really wanted: an explanation, a reason. Why had she stopped being my friend? It took a few weeks, but I finally got her to agree to take time out of her schedule to call me. I explained my concerns about her not calling or responding to my texts, and I even questioned her friendship. Her response this time dug a hole deeper into my heart: "We were never really friends anyway." She acted as if she was confused about why I was annoyed or even making this a big deal. I felt like a teenage girl with a crush, making a fool of herself begging a boy not to break up with her.

I realized in that moment that we had spent a lot of our lives together, but it was through church social events, including small groups and other ministries. We did not spend a ton of time together outside of those settings—though most of my close relationships are within those very settings. She made it clear that she was focusing on her business and her husband and was trying to figure out life. And I was not included. I ended that phone conversation more hurt and confused than I had started it. I expected a friend to apologize, ask for forgiveness, and maybe even argue with me, but not to walk away as if my life never mattered to her.

I would like to say that it was easy to forgive her and bless her. I am sure, however, that I carried unforgiveness in the depths of my heart for at least five years more before I was able to forgive her unconditionally. I continued to hear how she spent time with my other friends, which added to my hurt. I wanted them to defend me, stick up for me, confront her for excluding me. I had a difficult time knowing that other people were being treated *better* or *more fairly* than I was. She may not have intentionally treated me that way or even agreed with my perspective of this situation, but this is how my heart perceived that it happened.

Sometimes what we perceive is not always reality, an even more significant reason to forgive. I was waiting for an apology, an explanation, a reason. If I could have gotten one of them, then I felt I could have processed the forgiveness. But I waited for something that I would never get and something I did not have a right to demand. Colossians 3:13 reminds us, "Bearing with one another, and forgiving one another, if anyone has a complaint against another; even as Christ forgave you, so you also *must do.*"

The Bible clearly states that we must forgive others so that God will forgive our sins. In Mark 11:25, Jesus tells us, "And whenever you stand praying, if you have anything against anyone, forgive him, that your Father in heaven may also forgive you your trespasses." This is reiterated in Matthew 6:14-15, "For if you forgive men their trespasses, your heavenly Father will also forgive you. But if you do not forgive men their trespasses, neither will your Father forgive your trespasses." This is very serious. I do not want any unforgiveness in my heart to affect or threaten the forgiveness of my own sins.

How would the parable of the good Samaritan have turned out if the Samaritan had walked in unforgiveness? Would he have stopped for the wounded man? I am sure we all have issues in our lives requiring greater or lesser forgiveness than my example. We all have painful life stories of being wronged, with no apology given or explanation provided. You may have experiences that are far more heartbreaking and traumatic than what I shared. You may have experienced firsthand rejection, racism, abuse, rape, or even the murder of a loved one. All of it requires forgiveness.

My sister and her husband own a moving business. Before they owned their truck, they rented them. Not long before I wrote this book, her husband had been refused business with a trucking company for no real reason, although it became clear that it was due to his race. A white truck owner simply told my brother-in-law, a black male, that he had the right to refuse him service. The truck owner was extremely belligerent and would not give him any other reason, even though my brother-in-law had already signed the contract for the truck and was on his way to the job site.

My brother-in-law was born and raised in Mississippi, and I am positive he has seen, heard, and witnessed his share of unjust racial issues. Yet, in the nearly fifteen years I have known him, I have never once heard him say anything race-related that is unforgiving, angry, or judgmental. He is genuinely the most caring and humble person I know. He left that encounter with dignity and honor. He forgave the man on the spot and went to another town to receive a truck for a job three hours away. Had he had any unforgiveness deep in his heart from childhood or even his young adult life, that experience would have turned out differently.

Unforgiveness may be one of the enemy's greatest traps in destroying your life. Jesus commands us to forgive, even though it may be one of the most difficult things to do. Perhaps that is because it is the most powerful gift God has given to us. Without God, forgiveness is impossible. We can only forgive with the strength, power, and presence of the Holy Spirit. Only God can help you truly forgive any and every offense, including very deep, personal injustice. In Matthew 18, Jesus shared about an unmerciful servant who does not forgive the debt of another, even after he is forgiven his own, more significant debt.

> Then his master, after he had called him, said to him, "You wicked servant! I forgave you all that debt because you begged me. Should you not also have had compassion on your fellow servant, just as I had pity on you?" And his master was angry, and delivered him to the torturers until he should pay all that was due to him. So My heavenly Father also will do to you if each of you, from his heart, does not forgive his brother his trespasses.
>
> Matthew 18:32-35

It is all debt. All offenses, insults, and injustice are debt. But unforgiveness imprisons our hearts and tortures our souls. When Peter asked Jesus how many times we should truly forgive someone, Jesus responded that no matter how terrible the debt, we are to forgive an impossible number of times. Not only are we to forgive, but also we are to love and pray for our enemies so that we stand out from the world.

## LEARN TO GRIEVE

Here is the deal. When it comes to the unforgivable, we must face it, admit it, and grieve it. Forgiving someone does not mean it did not happen. It does not mean it is okay. And it does not mean that you should not mourn for your loss. Forgiving simply means you are giving it to God and setting it at His feet to handle. Acknowledge it so that you can release it to Jesus. It is okay to talk about. To discuss. To expose. To unveil. Light expels darkness. Evil must be exposed. That is what Jesus did—and does—when He walked this earth.

Sometimes, when we hear that we need to "forgive and forget," we think we are being told to act like nothing happened. Unfortunately, many times that is what is being said. *Just forget it. Do not talk about it. If you do, you are a victim. Just move on with your life.* Jesus does not want us to act like a victim but a victor. A victor is someone who acknowledges the harm they have experienced, hands it over to Jesus, and walks in victory to help others receive healing as well.

Grieving can be the most healing gift God has given to us. We are familiar and comfortable speaking about mourning when it comes to the loss of a loved one. However, in the world we live in, we need to give ourselves the permission to mourn when unjust things happen to us. You may have experienced the loss of a life, purity, financial security, dignity, or basic human equality. Post-traumatic stress disorder (PTSD) is known to result from a terrifying or traumatic event. I am not a doctor, but I would suggest that when PTSD occurs among soldiers who witness the most tragic events, the lack of ability or time taken to properly mourn and process the loss they experienced greatly contributes to the condition.

A friend of mine told me that her husband lost his best friend in the most traumatic way, involving a bomb. Rather than grieve the loss of his friend, he had to instantly move into a defensive stance to protect and strike back. It was shocking. It was unexpected. It was horrific and tragic. The PTSD he suffered after that was tremendous. I am sure you, your family, or friends can identify with this story. Without diminishing the seriousness of PTSD or the honor due our brave men and women who protect this country, I would like to make a loose analogy to the tragedies we face in life when we do not allow ourselves to genuinely grieve. It can be difficult for a mother who has lost her young child to leukemia to watch a special on television about a family losing a child to cancer. It can be hard on an adult who saw his mother abused to watch a movie with domestic violence. It can be difficult to experience a miscarriage and then hear about an abortion. It can be difficult, but we must grieve.

It is similar for the generation of people, including our parents and grandparents, that experienced firsthand hatred and racism in the form of lynching, church arson, and killings. It was shocking, horrible, tragic. Those same feelings of mental and emotional pain are revisited, and hearing "get over it" does not heal them but devalues their pain even more. We do not tell one mother who suffered the loss of a child to a drunk driver to "get over it" simply because another mother who suffered the same loss was able to recover faster. Thank God He gives us the ability to heal and recover from tragedy while here on Earth. We need to have compassion for the life experiences of others to help them completely heal and walk in forgiveness. If you have not allowed yourself to mourn the loss of something taken from you, know that God hears you. Remember His promise?

> To comfort all who mourn, to console those who mourn in Zion, to give them beauty for ashes, the oil of joy for mourning, the garment of praise for the spirit of heaviness; that they may be called trees of righteousness, the planting of the LORD, that He may be glorified. And they shall rebuild the old ruins, they shall raise up the former desolations, and they shall repair the ruined cities, the desolations of many generations.
>
> Isaiah 61:2-4

God loves you too much to leave you ruined, devastated, and in mourning. He wants to restore and rebuild you. Face the transgression, mourn the ashes, and give it to God to rebuild you.

## PRAY FOR YOUR ENEMY

Forgiveness gives you the power to do something about the evil. When women and children are trafficked, we must do something to expose the evil. When genocide occurs, we must expose the evil. When executives launder a company's assets, we must expose the evil. The victims themselves must forgive the harm they have received so they are not entangled with unforgiveness and offense in their own hearts after facing the reality of the trauma or tragedy.

Though it is not always the case, nor even conditional, offenders who are brought to justice in these tragic examples should also be given a chance, if they are willing, to receive reconciliation. This may be hard to accept, but look at the greater power of restoration. Imagine a woman trafficked into the disgusting sex arena. It is an honorable thing that, out of her freedom, she returns to set other women free. It is heroic should she choose to help set the oppressors free.

Most of us would want them to rot in hell (and I am there with you, most days), but how many of us have cried out to God to set free those who are tormented by the demonic realm and then curse them when we see them on the news? What is more impactful: to break one slave out in secret, or to break the slave owner free of his dark influence so he can, in turn, set the plantation free?

Pray for the oppressor. Hate the evil. Hate the injustice. Hate the darkness. It is good work to put an end to it. Keep in mind that doing the good work includes having forgiveness for all people. It is forgiveness that allows you to witness to their broken hearts and reconcile them from an eternity in hell.

Imagine the impact for the Kingdom of God if we attempted to reconcile more often with people who live in darkness. Imagine a heavy political power in our country that uses their national agenda to torment, kill, steal, and destroy all that is valuable to you. Considering the sensitive political environment we live in today, you may feel you are able to name that political power. But remember, the apostle Paul murdered Christians before he became an apostle. He enjoyed finding Christians and killing them.

Think about what this means to you. Really. What if President Obama or President Trump actually sought to kill you? You, specifically. Look what God did with Paul and the impact he had on our world. Two-thirds of the New Testament was written by him. The book many stand on for faith, guidance, and hope was co-written by a murderer. If the early Christians had decided to ruin him or kill him instead of forgiving him, where would we be? Pray for your enemy—the tormented and tormentor—as they are being held captive by the darkness.

> The servant of the Lord must not participate in quarrels, but must be kind to everyone [even-tempered, preserving peace, and he must be] skilled in teaching, patient *and* tolerant when wronged. He must correct those who are in opposition with courtesy *and* gentleness in the hope that God may grant that they will repent and be led to the knowledge of the truth [accurately understanding and welcoming it], and that they may come to their senses and *escape* from the trap of the devil, having been held captive by him to do his will.
>
> 2 Timothy 2:24-26 AMP

Have you been marked or beaten? Have you been discriminated against or treated unfairly? Have you experienced injustice? If so, consider yourself a servant of Christ. The servant is not better than the master. Isaiah 53:3 says, "He is despised and rejected by men, a Man of sorrows and acquainted with grief. And we hid, as it were, *our* faces from Him; He was despised, and we did not esteem Him." Jesus knows exactly how you feel. But you, also, can identify with Christ as Christ identifies with you and the injustices of the world. He was mobbed, beaten, spat on, rejected, called a liar, betrayed, abused, and murdered. He died for billions who would continue to reject Him even today. Christ knows your pain. Jesus prayed on the cross for the very people mocking, crucifying, and opposing Him: "Father, forgive them, for they do not know what they do" (Luke 23:34).

Like Christ, we also need to walk in a position of forgiving those who offend and reject us. An offense happened with someone in a book study, and afterward my sister reminded me that even Jesus' disciples betrayed Him after spending three intimate years with Him. Why would I think I would be treated any differently when the enemy wants to cause discord? Pray, forgive, release, and move on. I am sure I gave more time to the offense of that situation than I should have, but I know prayer and forgiveness helped keep my angry heart from becoming hard. We need to forgive everyone who hurts us, including parents, the church, another race, siblings, police, the President, or political parties. As Christians, we have to be leading examples of forgiveness. Forgiving a family member who abused you, a friend who betrayed you, or a boss who discriminated against you requires the same spiritual principle God demands be applied to those who commit prejudice, murder, racism, and injustice. It is all a debt that must be laid down at His feet.

Are you truly willing to forgive the unforgivable? What is unforgivable to you? An abusive father? A drunk driver who killed a child? A negligent doctor? An adulterous spouse? A racist police officer? A God that allowed your family member to suffer cancer? A rapist? A prejudiced government official? What does it look like to forgive these people?

One day, while journaling, I saw a vision of a mountain of garbage. It represented debt—my debt. In the vision, I was also holding bags and bags of garbage in my hands. It represented the hurt I experienced from others. Though the specific debts done to me may not have been the same offenses I carried out, the bags in my hands could not measure up to my mountain of debt owed to God. God had forgiven my mountain; therefore, I could not remind Him of the bags I was carrying in my hand. I had to choose to either carry them with me or lay them down once and for all.

Recognize that you might have some unforgiveness, anger, and hatred deep down in your own heart and it is time to lay it down. Think about it. Who do you know in your *mind* that you need to forgive but your *heart* has not allowed it? We cannot say we love God when we truly have unforgiveness and hatred in our hearts for those here on Earth. "If anyone says, I love God, and hates (detests, abominates) his brother [in Christ], he is a liar; for he who does not love his brother, whom he has seen, cannot love God, Whom he has not seen" (1 John 4:20 AMPC).

Even though God freed the Israelites from the unjust slavery of Egypt, many of them never left slavery behind. They were still enslaved in their minds. Unfortunately, they had to wander in the desert for forty years for a journey that should have only taken days. Only two out of the original two million Israelites made it into the Promised Land simply because of their mindsets. Who in this generation will make it past the ancestry of slavery, racism, and social injustice with forgiveness and compassion for a reconciled tomorrow?

## PREJUDGE

In addition to examining our hearts for unforgiveness, we also need to discover if we are carrying any judgment. We all have found ourselves in a position of judging someone, unfounded or not. As we have seen, however, the Scripture is clear about judgment: "Judge not, that you be not judged. For with what judgment you judge, you will be judged; and with the measure you use, it will be measured back to you" (Matthew 7:1-2). The judgment referred to here is not critical discernment between right and wrong, but a hypocritical and condemning attitude, looking down on another in order to make yourself feel better.

In that same passage in Matthew, Jesus also shared that we should consider our own shortcomings before judging others. Unfortunately, Christians can be incredibly judgmental toward others, confusing morality and correction with judgment and tearing others down. When you see a homeless man on the side of the street, it is easy to prejudge that he made bad choices or assume he is on drugs. When you see a shapely female walk into church with an outfit fit for the dance club, it may be tempting to judge her as loose. The scary part is, Jesus said that the same standard we use to judge will be used on us. He then said to pull the plank out of our own eye because we all fall short no matter how righteous we think we are.

Do not speak evil of one another, brethren. He who speaks evil of a brother and judges his brother, speaks evil of the law and judges the law. But if you judge the law, you are not a doer of the law but a judge. There is one Lawgiver, who is able to save and to destroy. Who are you to judge another?

James 4:11-12

If you do not deal with judgment, you will find yourself pre-judging others, which is a slippery slope that can develop into prejudice. When I was younger, I was taught that to pre-judge could lead to pre-judice, and pre-judice to pre-justice; or in other words, our judgement leads to prejudice, which leads to a lack of justice. According to Merriam Webster, stereotypes include unfair or untrue beliefs about people with particular characteristics. Judgment can develop into stereotyping others, which can lead to prejudice, which can produce discrimination or racism. Stereotyping is a kind of judgment that makes fun of another's inability or shortcomings. It's the kind of judgment that presumes the character of another based on clothing or speech, the kind of judgment that assumes the worst about someone's character due to their gender, race, or financial status.

James 3:10 says that blessings and curses cannot come out of the same mouth. We cannot call ourselves followers of Christ and then use ill words or have prejudice in our hearts toward another. If you find yourself categorizing another people group in a negative way, you need to honestly evaluate your heart. Do you have hatred, anger, or prejudice rooted deep in your heart? Have you referenced a race or culture in a statement of condemnation? Have you referred to another race or ethnicity as lazy, ignorant, bad drivers, stupid, illegal, gang members, or not good enough? Maybe you've never spoken anything out loud in a crowd of people, but what about to your spouse, best friend, or in your mind? Have you ever started a sentence with the phrase "Those people always . . ."?

There are people in your life who make mistakes, yourself included. We tend to judge others based on their actions in one area of their life, allowing it to overshadow what great accomplishments they made in other areas of life. It is easy for us to judge the issues we see or hear about on the news or social media with a political party, a pastor, or a race of people, without understanding who they truly are. We judge without seeing the whole picture. This is the state of our country right now and it is one of the reasons we are so divided. We can see the whole picture, or at least a bigger portion of it, when we remove ourselves from our own experiences for a moment and try to understand the experiences of someone else. Listening and honesty are what bring unity.

In Galatians 2, Paul rebuked Peter, one of Jesus' original disciples, for hypocrisy and racial pride. We have all sinned; we have all fallen short. In order to reconcile this nation, we need to admit if we have some form of judgment, prejudice, or hatred in our hearts toward other people or people groups. Then we need to repent to Jesus. You cannot truly live a life pleasing to God if you have any kind of hatred in your heart, whether it is toward a family member who has sinned against you or prejudice toward another race (see 1 John 2:9-11). Also, we cannot show favoritism to a particular culture, race, or people group. Whites cannot favor whites. Officers cannot favor officers. Blacks cannot favor blacks. People need to favor people.

> But the wisdom that is from above is first pure, then peaceable, gentle, willing to yield, full of mercy and good fruits, without partiality and without hypocrisy. Now the fruit of righteousness is sown in peace by those who make peace.
>
> James 3:17-18

Ask God if there is any prejudice, judgment, or racism that you need to deal with. I challenge you to ask God to examine and reveal anything rooted in your heart that needs to be released, exposed, or even replanted. I love Ezekiel 36:26 as our guide. Let's ask the Holy Spirit to convict our hearts now of any area of unforgiveness and prejudice and move us to a place of compassion and reconciling relationships.

# OVERCOMING OFFENSE

**An offended friend is harder to win back than a fortified city. Arguments separate friends like a gate locked with bars.**

PROVERBS 18:19 NLT

We can all identify with being offended at some point in our lives. We currently live in a world where almost everyone around us is extremely easy to offend. We walk in offense as a nation, as a culture, as a church, and as individuals. Our offense is one of the biggest obstacles to resolving our differences and reconciling our nation. Offense was an obstacle the Samaritan had to overcome before he could help the wounded man. It is an obstacle we must overcome before we can move forward in unity.

The Greek word for "offense" is *skandalon*. It is also where we get the word "scandal" from. It means the bait of a trap, a snare, or a stumbling block. Does that sound about right to you? When we are living in offense and we reflect on where things went wrong in our hearts, we can typically pinpoint it back to just that: a snare. You are bait. I am bait. We are all bait for the stumbling blocks of this world to snare us up in offense. When we become offended and don't recognize it or don't do anything about it, we become a victim. We are all potential victims if we allow ourselves to remain in the trap.

Racism is a trap. Discrimination is a stumbling block. Prejudice is bait. It is natural to get offended when we are insulted, especially if the insult has to do with our race, gender, or any other situation into which we were born. If we get offended when someone says they don't like our outfit, how much more offended will we get if someone condemns something about us over which we have no control? What unique characteristic do you have that others have mocked? Do you have a large nose? Big ears? Wild hair? Small eyes? Freckles? Did the mockery cause you to build a sensitivity to the very feature or characteristic that makes you unique?

When we become overly sensitive about our characteristics or features, it is tempting to live in an alarmed state of emotion, assuming people are treating us differently because of that very thing. If you are used to covering your teeth when you laugh, and someone looks at your mouth before you move your hand, then perhaps you assume they are judging your teeth. If you have a lazy eye and someone looks into your eyes, you may feel like they are examining you. Sometimes when we are so used to being picked on, insulted, or offended, we become a victim. We are so used to offense that we encounter it everywhere, and we convince ourselves that it is never our fault.

There are many other ways we get snared by offense. Have you ever said the phrase "My pet peeve is..."? Merriam Webster defines a pet peeve as "a frequent subject of complaint." Other sources describe a pet peeve as a minor annoyance, something that might not bother everyone but it bothers you. We all have them, minor annoyances or complaints. Shoes left in front of the door. Empty cereal boxes placed back in the pantry. Gum popping. These seem innocent and simple. However, we have to be careful not to allow even small, simple annoyances to establish a root of offense in our hearts.

What pet peeves or offensive traps have you allowed yourself to walk into? Merriam Webster also defines "annoyance" as "a source of vexation or irritation." The book of James tells us how an infant temptation can turn into a full-grown sin, bringing death, if we are not careful to check our hearts (see James 1:14-15). In this case, a small annoyance can lead to irritation, which can be a death trap of offense and victimhood.

## VICTIM MENTALITY

Victims point fingers. They blame others. They become more comfortable being a victim than fighting to be a victor. Why fight when we can blame someone else for our lack of success? Becoming a victim is much easier than we might think. Offense usually stems from a legitimate, unfortunate life circumstance, turning innocent, unsuspecting individuals into lifelong victims. At some point, most victims have a chance to fight their way out of woundedness and offense. We become trapped by a victim mentality when we choose to give in and not fight, letting the offense be our defense. You cannot defeat what you are not willing to confront.

I read an incredible book called *UnOffendable: No offense. None taken.* by writer, speaker, and filmmaker Ryan Leak. He teaches the principles of living an unoffendable life by overcoming the things that hurt us most, to shape our lives for the better. Coincidentally, after finishing the book, the very next day was one of the worst days I had experienced in a long time. I was offended all day long. The day started out with what I felt were very unrealistic goals presented by my boss. In my opinion, I had been beaten up all year, pushing myself to be creative in order to meet unfair expectations—the reality of a sales world. I am an extremely competitive person. My boss gave me the nickname "hunter-killer" for a reason. So, that day, when my boss challenged me about my lack of progress, I felt like my work ethic was being questioned, and I was livid. Instead of turning to God and praying to settle my spirit, I called and complained to not one but two coworkers. I carried an offended heart all day. I had a hard time shaking the heaviness. When I arrived at a lunch meeting, I got irritated with a rude waiter, so I matched his rudeness. When you have an offended spirit, your defensive spirit is also heightened.

Finally, I dragged myself into the last meeting of the day. I was drained and grew annoyed with the business partner as she complained and threatened to remove her personal account from me. I saw it as a threat, when in reality she was also just having a bad day. Her husband had died months earlier and she could no longer afford the account. She also had a migraine and her boss had just been yelling at her in the other room.

To end my day, I received an email from my son's teacher, alleging he was involved in a cheating coup that day. She had the audacity to call my son a cheater! Offended "mama bear" went into attack mode. I wrote the teacher a seven-paragraph dissertation, letting her have all of my offense, frustration, and disappointment. After talking to my son, I learned that after several attempts to hide his paper, he eventually gave in and allowed his buddy to copy his answers. I was glad in that moment that I had decided not to send the email.

When we're offended, our lenses are foggy and not clear. We view life through hurt eyes and not healed eyes. It is difficult to have compassion for someone else when you are concerned about your own hurts, when you're a victim. If I had approached my day from compassion instead of offense, I would not have reacted to the hard-working waiter who did not make enough money to deal with rude or slow customers during the lunch hustle. I would have chosen to see the teacher as the tired soul in charge of a classroom full of rambunctious boys who need to take responsibility for their actions. What would have happened had I continued to walk in offense not just for one day but the entire week, month, or even years? Some people live in victimhood from childhood; their whole lives are spent in offense and bitterness.

## THE BONDAGE OF SLAVERY

As I mentioned previously, I believe African Americans can be compared to the half-breed Samaritan. They are not completely African and not originally from America. They were taken from their homeland and intermingled with foreigners. They were a newly created race. History tells us African Americans were made to feel they did not belong to either place. They were not embraced in their native land or in their current land. Many experienced isolation and abandonment and felt rejected from both sides. Rejection is a trap similar in nature to offense. The power of rejection is real and alive, and I believe it has attached itself to many within the African-American race, preventing them from fully overcoming the bondage of slavery.

What does a slave look like? A slave is oppressed. A slave runs. A slave is fearful. A slave is not educated. A slave does not have tools to make wise decisions. A slave does not have value. A slave is beaten. A slave has no hope. Slavery is just as much a mentality as it is a physical entrapment. In America, the black community suffers the most from fatherlessness, single-parent homes, imprisonment, drugs, and gangs—more than any other community in the United States. Data shows that the odds are stacked against those raised in a single-parent home: there is a 48 percent chance that they will end up living in poverty. The odds are against some people before they are even born. If you watched your parents and grandparents struggle, what gives you hope that your life will be any different?

Clearly, historical oppression has negatively affected this people group. Have we, as a nation, acknowledged the consequences and afflictions caused by enslaving an entire people? Can we truly ignore the role slavery played in leading us to the oppressive social issues we face today?

Paul Sheppard, an African-American pastor originally from the East Coast who now leads a church in California, taught a great series on the story of Joseph in the Bible. Joseph was the youngest of his twelve brothers. He was also his father's favorite child, and his older siblings were extremely jealous over what they considered unfair treatment. Joseph worked at home and wore the best clothes while his brothers worked the hardest outdoor labor jobs. One day, his brothers conspired to kill him. One brother convinced the others to sell him into slavery instead. Joseph became a slave, then a prisoner, then—because of a God-given gift of wisdom—he ended up in Pharaoh's palace as his second in command.

Joseph was wrongly imprisoned, an act of injustice at its core. He had no rights as a slave. But God favored him, and he made his way to lead the entire land of Egypt in Pharaoh's name. I love what Paul Sheppard says in his message: "I'd rather be blessed than have my rights. Some things Jesse Jackson or Al Sharpton cannot do (or provide) for me. Sometimes I have to be discriminated against and trust God anyway. I'd rather have favor from God than fairness from man."

Throughout his message, Paul shares that we don't always get what we deserve in this world. However, God is on top of any ceiling holding you back or limiting you. If God is for you, no one can hold you back. Paul reminds us that nothing will change until hearts are changed, and so we must educate each other on the issues of today. We must not live like victims or blame "the man." Man doesn't have that much power. When we don't encounter justice, he encourages us to "go find God." Pastor Sheppard points out that it was God who let Joseph stay in jail for years, not man. God allows us to go through things in life that are unjust, but He will also reconcile, restore, and redeem us if we allow Him to.

By the end of his journey, Joseph is completely reconciled to his family, including his father, who believed him dead. Joseph was willing to forgive his brothers, letting go of victimhood. We have the opportunity to do the same thing. Any racial discrimination against you or your family is wrong. It is awful. It is a transgression. It is an iniquity. That said, you have to let God heal you and overcome any hurt or offense so that you do not pass on a slave mentality to the next generation.

The Hebrew people were enslaved for 400 years by the Egyptians. While they might have forgotten God during their physically, mentally, and emotionally abusive slave labor, God did not forget His people. In fact, God intentionally pursued them, reintroduced Himself, and reestablished a relationship with them. He promised them their inheritance; all they had to do was follow Him and have a relationship with Him. It took them forty years of freedom before they were able to receive the inheritance God had promised them.

He reestablished their throne, dominion, and their legacy in their new land—Israel.

Years later, God sent Jesus to Earth to permanently break every bondage of slavery here on Earth and for eternity. God sees our pains, our trials, our tribulations—and our slavery. He does not forget. He does return. He will reestablish what is rightfully yours, but you must not see yourself as a slave, act like a slave, or think like a slave. You are free. Galatians says to not return to bondage when God has set you free.

Receive your promise. Be who God called you to be. No matter the amount of oppression placed on your life or the lives of your ancestors, God wants you to break free of those chains and never return to slavery. You are an heir to the throne. Rise up and take your inheritance from your Father. As Ryan Leak reminds us in *Un-Offendable*, "do not let your history paralyze your destiny."

## LET GO OF THE GARBAGE

When I shared with a close friend my plan to memorialize my great-great-grandmother with the vase of cotton, she vehemently disagreed with my idea. I thought she would find some deep, spiritual meaning behind it, but she had the total opposite response. My friend felt like the cotton implied I was dwelling on the past. She reminded me that it is a dark time in our society, and I should not intentionally remind others of it. She also felt that the cotton did not represent who I am today or the success I've experienced in life. I think her real concern was that I would appear to be an angry, offended person of color. I listened and wondered, *What do other people of color feel like when they look at cotton or any symbol of slavery? Does it cause pain or anger? If a person is healed of the painful past and no longer carrying offense, would they react or respond the same way?*

God told the Israelites to create memorials and to tell their children's children the stories of how He brought them out of bondage. Slavery in America was a dark time. Today, we have an opportunity to give glory to God for what He delivered our people through. God said to remember where He brought us from, but not so that we can relive the pain, anger, and hatred. We remember so that we can tell the generations of His glory and teach them how to walk in freedom.

While my friend did not want the symbolic reminder of slaves picking cotton, I struggled with other emotional aspects of racial injustice. I had a hard time joining social justice conversations regarding African-American issues. My youngest sister, who lives in New York, would often want to discuss the unjust issues happening in our country. The topic brought me to a dark, emotional place. I did not want to hear what she had to say because it developed anger in me. I was angry for young black teens being killed, but I was also angry that all white police officers were being blamed. I was angry that a grieving mother was taken advantage of by social and political agendas. I was angry that extreme conservatives who claimed faith in God would be so cold about the innocent deaths. There are people being crushed by racism in the United States because there is a real darkness trying to steal and kill. It is real. But I knew that anger wouldn't solve the problem. There is a real enemy, but it is not each other.

Galatians 6:2 says, "Bear one another's *burdens*, and so fulfill the law of Christ . . ." and verse 5 says, "For each one shall bear his own *load*" (emphasis added). This may seem contradictory, but the meaning of "burden" that the author, apostle Paul, is speaking of in verse 2 is different from the meaning of "load" in verse 5. Biblical studies show us that the word "load" in this context is a weight that must be carried by the individual and cannot be transferred or shifted to someone else. The burden mentioned in verse 2, however, refers to an overwhelming burden or weight that is heavy and crushing. The author reminds us that there are individual burdens we are responsible to carry ourselves and that there are burdens too heavy to carry alone. While we can all help with the crushing burden of racism, we cannot carry someone else's load of offense, anger, or hatred. God asks us to help others when the load crushes them. Racism, hatred, and prejudice are crushing loads, and we need to step in and help those who are burdened by these realities.

> Finally, my brethren, be strong in the Lord and in the power of His might. Put on the whole armor of God, that you may be able to stand against the wiles of the devil. For we do not wrestle against flesh and blood, but against principalities, against powers, against the rulers of the darkness of this age, against spiritual hosts of wickedness in the heavenly places. Therefore take up the whole armor of God, that you may be able to withstand in the evil day, and having done all, to stand.
>
> Stand therefore, having girded your waist with truth, having put on the breastplate of righteousness, and having shod your feet with the preparation of the gospel of peace; above all, taking the shield of faith with which you will be able to quench all the fiery darts of the wicked one. And take the helmet of salvation, and the sword of the Spirit, which is the word of God.
>
> Ephesians 6:10-17

This Scripture in the New Testament, also written by the apostle Paul, clearly states that we do not fight against black, white, yellow, blue, or purple flesh. We fight against the spirit realm, another power, evil. We cannot fight in the courts, or on the streets, or even in our churches, if we don't start with truth, righteousness, peace, faith, salvation, prayer, and most powerful of all, the Word of God. Most fights we have do not include God's Word. Instead, we fight using our opinions, beliefs, and experiences. Even experiences can lack the whole picture. Only God's Word is complete truth. Martin Luther King, Jr. armed himself with just that when he protested, when he spoke at the White House, and when he sat in county jails. We cannot confuse fighting for social agendas with fighting for our own agendas. We have to start with God's agenda.

We all have pain from our past that comes in many shapes and sizes. Yours may be abuse or racism. Someone else may have pain from prejudice, fatherlessness, or abandonment. One day I read a particular passage in the Bible and a lightbulb went off in my soul that would change the course of my life forever. The passage helped me see that my brokenness leads to healing. The same applies to you. "It is good for me that I have been afflicted, that I may learn Your statutes. The law of Your mouth is better to me than thousands of coins of gold and silver" (Psalm 119:71-72). I love verse 71 as it appears in The Message even more: "My troubles turned out all for the best—they forced me to learn from your textbook."

It was clear to me maybe for the first time that I could take real joy in my pain and afflictions. They were good for me because they led me to God's mercy seat. My pain led me to His Word, and it was His Word that could do more for me than all of the silver and gold in the world. He alone is my strength. My pain brought me closer to my Father, and out of that would produce more wisdom, more riches, more glory, and more healing than if I had never experienced the pain. I am closer to my Father because of my afflictions, so I thank God for them. Because of my experiences, I can teach my children valuable lessons, encourage a friend in sorrow, or help someone to persevere through a crisis. I can only do those things with joy, peace, and laughter if I appreciate my past and not wallow in it. I can only set others free if I am free.

What I experienced in that moment was the Holy Spirit giving me complete freedom from my past. I had an earth-breaking and heaven-shaking revelation. God's light became my shining armor, not the darkness. I knew it was time to look to my future and not my past. I had to consider what lies I was believing, causing me to stumble and live in my past instead of my present. Was I holding onto my past more than I was holding onto God? The hurt? The pain? It was time to release it like the garbage it was. It was time to turn my face to look at God's glory instead. It was done. It was over. It was released. My past is my past.

In order to walk into my future without my past stringing along, I had to declare that I trusted God with my future more than I feared my past. You cannot walk forward while looking backward and holding onto the garbage of the past. It's time to set it down. If you let it, the pain of your past allows you to seek God and know Him, love Him, and be known by Him. It allows you to encourage others to seek their Father in heaven. To accept His love. To get rid of their pain.

My past has given me a chance to laugh, be creative, appreciate diversity, love my family, seek God's Word, have compassion, give great hugs, celebrate lives, seek truth, pursue knowledge and wisdom, work hard, really love my boys, encourage marriages, seek wholeness, serve at church, sing loudly and worship with joy, seek peace, seek life without fear, and please and love my Father. My life is better because of what I experienced and endured from childhood to adulthood, and every bitter or sweet obstacle in between. If we allow it, the pain and hurts of life can be overshadowed by God's grace, goodness, and love. One of the greatest gifts of pain is that it teaches us how to help lessen the pain of another.

## IRON SHARPENS IRON

Think of your five closest friends. Think about the individuals with whom you spend most of your time communicating, texting, or doing life. Do you feel comfortable enough in your relationships to point out a friend's flaw or an error, or even a different opinion, without offending them? Do they feel comfortable enough to approach you and share absolutely anything about you or your life without offending you? Before you answer this, really stop and consider it. If your friend or family member told you they did not agree with you buying another vehicle due to your financial circumstances, what would you say? Do you truly feel comfortable telling your friend that her children are complete brats and she needs to discipline them better? Are you okay with your friend telling you that you are too busy for your family and need to get your priorities straight? Have you ever opened the door for *that* conversation?

We like to think we are above offense, that we would easily give and receive constructive feedback. When we evaluate our hearts, we often find a different reality. When was the last time you gave or received honest wisdom? If your family shared constructive feedback, would you fly off the handle? Ignore them? Talk about them? It feels vulnerable to open our heart to others, but even the Bible tells us to seek wise counsel. God put relationships in our lives to sharpen us so that we would receive wisdom in our inner being. In Psalm 51:6, King David wrote, "Behold, You desire truth in the inner being; make me therefore to know wisdom in my inmost heart." God put family and friends in our lives to encourage and correct us, and it is our job to open our hearts to receive from them.

Are you open to feedback in your marriage from your spouse? For your business from a partner or financial planner? As a pastor from your leadership team? As a father from your children? The Bible clearly tells us that a friend who is willing to tell us the truth is better than an enemy who lies to us. It also speaks of iron sharpening iron. This sounds full of wisdom when we quote it; however, have you ever seen two swords or knives being sharpened? Sparks fly. There is an awful sound of clanging metal. It is not pleasant, but it is necessary.

How many of your relationships allow for sparks to fly, for iron to sharpen iron? Sadly, most of us won't be able to answer that question. It is not about being rude, but honest. Just like medicine, the truth can hurt, but it allows for healing. If you had a friend who was about to drive his car off a ledge, and he did not know it, would you warn him? Do you notify oncoming traffic of the officer waiting around the corner for them? Do you remind strangers of the spill on the floor?

We do not allow our friends and family, whom we love and know intimately, to drive head-on into danger because we are too scared to be honest with them. Except we do almost every day. I have a group of trusted, experienced, and wise women in my life, in addition to my husband, whom I openly ask to give me feedback and direction in the decisions I make. And I am still learning how to take feedback. It took me fifteen years to get to a place where I could allow my husband to openly and honestly speak truth to me without my feelings getting in the way. Now I cannot imagine a life where we don't honestly and openly share our deepest feelings and thoughts with one another.

Early in our marriage, I had an epiphany that James and I were not being good friends to another family. We felt they were making unwise choices, and instead of addressing it we chose to judge them. We shook our heads at them, criticizing them in our hearts and in our discussions. When we share and sharpen out of love, it ultimately brings healing. James and I agreed that we needed to be better, more courageous friends. An opportunity presented itself and my husband had a tough conversation with the friend about how he treated his family. It allowed the friend to reflect on his life and behavior. Whether or not he chose to change his behavior was not up to us. It was our responsibility, however, to be honest and truthful and to continue to love that friend regardless of the outcome. Thankfully, that conversation led to healed relationships within the family.

It has to start with us. We have to be better friends to those in our circles of influence. We need to show the world how to accept feedback without becoming offended, otherwise the cycle will continue of an overly sensitive, divided nation that is not open to honesty. There are times we share truth with family and friends, and it ends a relationship. When we are harsh with our honesty, it causes fear, not reconciliation. Other times, we do not say anything at all and slowly distance ourselves, which also can end a relationship. The message of Jesus Christ is truth and grace—not just grace, and not just truth, but both. An honest look at our hearts, our motives, and our actions will provide an open door to healing in our homes, marriages, and society.

Less than twenty-four hours from typing the first draft of this chapter, I had an opportunity to walk this principal out. I made a lighthearted joke to a friend in a group text and she sent me a separate text asking me to remove it. I thought her text was short and rude—not that I could actually tell her tone through a text. It was unexpected. She rejected my humor, and I felt like she also rejected *me. How dare she?* I thought. *It was no big deal! Why is she so sensitive? I am never joking with her again. Is she even my friend?* As innocent as I'd like to sound, all of those feelings and more rushed through my head within a split second. I felt humiliated that she would question my character and I wanted to defend myself. I flirted with offense, not because she was wrong, but because she made me feel bad.

I was offended that I had offended her. And further, she had the audacity to tell me about myself. Well, exactly. She had the audacity, courage, and character to tell me about myself. When that realization hit me, I humbled myself immediately (well, immediately may be relative in God's time, but in human time it was pretty quick), apologized, and told her I would remove the text. Instead of being offended with me due to my joke, she told me she really appreciated my response and my friendship. It was not what I was expecting. I was expecting to get a short text back or nothing at all, since I thought I had offended her.

See, many times we play defense with our offense. We use our offense against another to defend our insulted hearts. "I am offended that you are offended with me!" we cry. In that moment with my friend, I made up my mind that I needed to rid my heart of offense or it would seep into my life and potentially ruin my friendship. I thanked her for opening up with such courage, still loving me and not continuing to judge me after that incident. That is a true friend. I finished my day happier than I started it. A friend was brave enough to confront me about my tongue, and I was willing to receive it (though my flesh did struggle), and we both walked away with love, grace, and a deeper appreciation of our friendship.

## KNOW WHO YOU ARE

Another way to stay out of the trap of offense is by knowing who you are. Genesis 1:26-27 reads:

> Then God said, "Let Us make man in Our image, according to Our likeness; let them have dominion over the fish of the sea, over the birds of the air, and over the cattle, over all the earth and over every creeping thing that creeps on the earth." So God created man in His *own* image; in the image of God He created him; male and female He created them.

We are made in the image of God according to His likeness and His character. What is God like? His character traits include love, patience, forgiveness, hope, faithfulness, and unity. God displays unity in this Scripture, including the Trinity and making man in "Our image." Men and women are not distinguished here because they both are equally made in God's image and given power and dominion over the earth, not each other. Through life's circumstances many of us walk in a limiting view of ourselves because of an underprivileged title placed on us by this world's dominating forces. Instead, we must accept the identity God gave us over the identity with which man tries to limit us.

On July 7, 2016, there was a deadly police shooting in Dallas, Texas. The shooting was led by an Army Reserve Afghan war veteran who was reportedly angry over the police-involved deaths of young black males in Baton Rouge, Louisiana, and Falcon Heights, Minnesota. He killed five police officers and injured nine others. We have friends who serve within the Dallas Police Department who lost loved ones that day. It was a tragic day in Dallas, just like it had been in Baton Rouge and Falcon Heights. Any loss of innocent life is a tragedy.

This is an example of someone with a limited perspective of offense taking the justice of this world into his own hands. Priscilla Shirer, an African-American author, evangelist, and actress, resides in Dallas with her family. She spoke on this issue later that year at a women's event. She discussed that her true identity as God's child came before a temporary label of her race, or even her gender. Her primary identity is as a child of God, and that usurped any earthly title. Galatians 3:26-29 reads:

> For you are all sons of God through faith in Christ Jesus. For as many of you as were baptized into Christ have put on Christ. There is neither Jew nor Greek, there is neither slave nor free, there is neither male nor female; for you are all one in Christ Jesus. And if you *are* Christ's, then you are Abraham's seed, and heirs according to the promise.

This Scripture is pretty clear that we wear Christ's identity and not our temporary earthly identities. If you live your life defined by a temporary label like gender, race, or sexuality, then you are limiting your true identity. You have a higher identity. When you define yourself first by the temporary titles of this world, then you are more prone to offend or be offended when your title or label conflicts with someone else's title. The titles we live by today will be gone the moment we leave this earth; they die with us.

This Scripture tells us that we are one in Christ, Abraham's seed. That is our true identity. Anything less is just that: less. If you are a Christian, you cannot allow racism, or sexism, or any other division to impact the way you see others, because Christ sees you, them, us as one. He sees Himself in you. He is not dividing us into separate boroughs in heaven. We are not separated as men and women, black and white, poor and rich, Republican or Democrat. Heaven will not separate left hands from the right ankle, or the right knee from the left pinky toe. We will enter as one body. We will enter in as the image of God.

Who have you excluded in your heart, church, community, or workplace because you were looking at their temporary identity? How have you limited yourself by identifying with a temporary or secondary identity? Whether you have been limiting others by their earthly identities or you are offended that others have done that to you, it is time to step away from looking horizontally at each other and look vertically to God. No one is limited by man's sinful divisions. Instead, we are unlimited in Christ's unified image. It is time to unite through Jesus. It is time to recognize who you are.

A friend of mine told me that her son overheard his minority football teammate being called a *nigger* by a white player on the opposing team. He was shocked at the racial insult, but even more so by his teammate's response. The older teammate walked away in silence. When my friend's son asked the older boy why he did not retaliate or get mad, the teammate responded, "That wasn't the first time and it won't be the last time." That wise young man understands his higher identity and made up his mind that no matter what his enemy calls him, he will not listen or respond. He knows who he is and is not.

In Matthew 15, Jesus shared the story of the woman who refused to be offended. She was a Gentile, but Jesus' ministry was not focused on Gentiles at the time. Despite that, the woman pleaded with Jesus to heal her sick daughter.

But He answered her not a word. And His disciples came and urged Him, saying, "Send her away, for she cries out after us." But He answered and said, "I was not sent except to the lost sheep of the house of Israel." Then she came and worshiped Him, saying, "Lord, help me!" But He answered and said, "It is not good to take the children's bread and throw it to the little dogs." And she said, "Yes, Lord, yet even the little dogs eat the crumbs which fall from their masters' table."

Matthew 15:23-27

At first, the woman was rejected by the disciples. They were annoyed with her. They looked down on her and even asked Jesus to send her away. Imagine her rejection and her initial offense. But she persisted. Perhaps she hoped that even though man told her no, God Himself might tell her yes. When she went in to request healing from Jesus, the source of all healing, He called her a dog. Ouch. Jews called Gentiles *dog* as a derogatory remark. Instead of getting offended, she humbled herself. She moved past the insult in order to seek true life and healing. She refused to let an offensive word keep her from the blessing of healing and freedom for her daughter. "Then Jesus said to her, 'Woman, you have great faith! Your request is granted.' And her daughter was healed at that moment" (Matthew 15:28).

Jesus did not believe she was a dog; He was simply testing her faith and perseverance. Imagine if she had walked away in offense with a victimized spirit. What would have happened to her and her daughter? When we are easily triggered by offense, we opt out of the healing Jesus Christ provides for us and for our families. When you know who you truly are, however, you have no need to be offended by prejudiced words spoken against you. Have we allowed our offenses to disrupt or get us off track from what our true blessing, calling, power, and healing can be for ourselves and for our legacy? Jesus told the woman she had great faith. Her choice to believe—and her refusal to get offended—was attributed to her as faith. Let's also be known by our faith and not our offense.

> And Jesus called [to Him] the throng with His disciples and said to them, If anyone intends to come after Me, let him deny himself [forget, ignore, disown, and lose sight of himself and his own interests] and take up his cross, and [joining Me as a disciple and siding with My party] follow with Me [continually, cleaving steadfastly to Me].
>
> For whoever wants to save his [higher, spiritual, eternal] life, will lose it [the lower, natural, temporal life which is lived only on earth]; and whoever gives up his life [which is lived only on earth] for My sake and the Gospel's will save it [his higher, spiritual life in the eternal kingdom of God].
>
> Mark 8:34-35 AMPC

It is time to give up your lower, temporal image to replace it with your higher, eternal image: a child of God. Your culture or your race cannot sit on the throne, only God can. Put your hope in Jesus. He died to sit on the throne for you and will restore you from your offenders just as He will restore His Kingdom.

## GIVE IT TO GOD

It is easy to walk in offense when you feel or believe that no one sees you, or that no one cares. Offense comes so easily when you believe that you will not be restored or receive restitution for what has been stolen from you. In the story of Joseph, before he received any restitution or redemption for being sold into slavery by his brothers, he chose to give his offenses and pain to God. In turn, God gave Joseph enough provision to care for his entire family and restored his relationship with his brothers and father. Refuse to let offense inhibit you. Instead, give your issues to God. He sees the oppression. He has not forgotten you. He will redeem you. Put your hope in the Lord. God, and God alone, can redeem and restore you and your family as He did for Joseph.

> For He will deliver the needy when he cries, the poor also, and him who has no helper. He will spare the poor and needy and will save the souls of the needy. He will redeem their life from oppression and violence; and precious shall be their blood in His sight.
>
> Psalm 72:12-14

God sees the poor, the underdog, the underprivileged. He sees the forsaken, the abandoned, and the abused. He will redeem them from the hatred, discrimination, and lack of value they have endured. The blood that has been shed, the sacrifices made—it is all valued in heaven. It has not gone to waste and has a high price in God's eyes.

Proverbs 14:31 issues a warning to those who oppress others: "He who oppresses the poor reproaches his Maker, but he who honors Him has mercy on the needy." A similar warning appears in Zechariah 7:10: "Do not oppress the widow or the fatherless, the alien or the poor. Let none of you plan evil in his heart against his brother." God hates racism, oppression, and injustice. Christ cares for you just as He cared for His Hebrew nation that was oppressed and in captivity in Egypt.

Then they cried out to the LORD in their trouble, and He saved them out of their distresses. He brought them out of darkness and the shadow of death and broke their chains in pieces. . . . When they are diminished and brought low through oppression, affliction, and sorrow, He pours contempt on princes, and causes them to wander in the wilderness where there is no way; yet He sets the poor on high, far from affliction, and makes their families like a flock. The righteous see it and rejoice, and all iniquity stops its mouth.

Psalm 107:13-14, 39-42

As black slaves read this passage, it gave them the hope to break out of their chains. It is the same hope you have been given to break free of the bondage of social injustice today. If you have seen oppression and injustice, be glad, as it makes you like our Savior as He was oppressed and afflicted (see Isaiah 53:7). The good news is that the Lord executes righteousness and justice for all who are oppressed (see Psalm 103:6) and God will restore what you have lost.

In April 2018 I went to Washington, DC, and attended a tour at the Museum of the Bible. It was an incredible experience and I am convinced it would take an entire week of eight-hour days to experience everything in the museum. On one floor there are historical Bibles from all over the world, including a historical Samaritan Bible and scrolls. It was here that the tour guide showed us Bibles that were given to slaves in America. He shared with us that many black slaves were, in fact, allowed to read the Bible. These Bibles were referred to as "slave Bibles." Tragically, according to the exhibit, the slave Bible is missing approximately 90 percent of the Old Testament and 50 percent of the New Testament. Compared to the 1,189 chapters in a standard Protestant Bible, the slave Bible contains only 232. Some of the missing books are Psalms, Exodus, Mark, Esther, Romans, and Revelation. Most of these books can be summed up as offering hope and a future for the oppressed.

Exodus specifically outlines God rescuing the slaves. The hope that God saw their oppression, their pain, and their injustice was stolen from the Word of God and the hearts of American slaves. Maybe worse, the absence of that book would cause the slaves to question whether or not God agreed with slavery or even truly cared to save them. Many today may feel the same way: that the lack of hope for the black community displays how God feels about them. However, these books, including Exodus, should give us all hope to turn to God in times of oppression and offense. Exodus 2:23-25 reads:

> Now it happened in the process of time that the king of Egypt died. Then the children of Israel groaned because of the bondage, and they cried out; and their cry came up to God because of the bondage. So God heard their groaning, and God remembered His covenant with Abraham, with Isaac, and with Jacob. And God looked upon the children of Israel, and God acknowledged them.

Later, in Exodus 3, God called to Moses to lead His people out of slavery: "And the LORD said: 'I have surely seen the oppression of My people who are in Egypt, and have heard their cry because of their taskmasters, for I know their sorrows. So I have come down to deliver them out of the hand of the Egyptians'" (vv. 7-8).

Brothers and sisters, God has seen the oppression on your lives, in your neighborhoods, at your schools. He has not forsaken you.

He has not forgotten you. He will deliver you, your children, and your community just as He did His people in Israel. You are the seed of Abraham; therefore, you, too, are His child and receive the same promises. God is your savior, not man. Exodus 4:31 tells us how the Hebrew slaves responded to their freedom: "So the people believed; and when they heard that the LORD had visited the children of Israel and that He had looked on their affliction, then they bowed their heads and worshiped."

Remind yourself to worship and thank God for His protection. He is coming for you just as He came for the children of Israel. God is your provider, healer, peace, shepherd, and defender. He loves you, sees you, and knows your pain. He will not allow you to stay defeated or oppressed. He has provided you with freedom and liberty! Trust Him to break the yoke of bondage.

In the story of Job, we are reminded of the travesties in life we experience that make us question God's love for us. The book of Job describes a level of suffering that most of us are not willing to take the time to read about. It is difficult to intentionally read through the pain and tragedy of a life like Job's. So much was taken from him: he endured disease to his body and the loss of his family and all of his riches. We may know people in our own lives who have experienced similar catastrophe. At the end of Job, after God made it clear that He is the one who set the stars in the sky, He blessed Job doubly. God saw Job as a righteous man. Job had character and integrity. After receiving a double blessing from God, Job turned around and gave equal inheritance to both his sons *and* to his daughters. Do you understand how important that was? He set the example to the generations that followed, demonstrating that we should embrace generosity and equality as we show thankfulness for God's blessings.

Job lost everything. His family. His health. His legacy. His possessions. And to make it worse, his only friends insulted and criticized him. If anyone had permission to be offended or to feel like a victim, it was Job. However, after God rebuked him and then extended mercy, Job repented. Then God asked Job to pray for the very friends who insulted him and blamed him for his own mishaps in life. Are there people in your life who blame you for your mishaps? Are you insulted by others who claim that what you wear, what you do, or what you look like contributes to your own negative experiences in life? Stand up, like Job, and proclaim, "For I know that my Redeemer lives, and He shall stand at last on the earth" (Job 19:25).

Take note when and how God restores Job in verses 42:10-12:

And the LORD restored Job's losses when he prayed for his friends. Indeed the LORD gave Job twice as much as he had before. Then all his brothers, all his sisters, and all those who had been his acquaintances before, came to him and ate food with him in his house; and they consoled him and comforted him for all the adversity that the LORD had brought upon him. . . . Now the LORD blessed the latter days of Job more than his beginning.

Job's restoration came only after he prayed for the very men who contributed to his pain, insulted his integrity, and judged his life. For those who have been unjustly hurt, oppressed, and punished, God will be faithful to you just like He was to Job. God is our defender. Pray for your enemy.

Jesus is also your Healer—not just from sickness and disease, but also from an offended and oppressed heart. When Jesus walked this earth, His ministry was anointed with the Holy Spirit and He "healed all who were oppressed" (Acts 10:38). We think of a healed broken ankle or a broken marriage but what about a broken identity or heart when it comes to racial and social injustice issues? Are we willing to place those on the altar as much as our salvation or addiction to alcohol or drugs? Oppression in any format needs to be placed on the altar for Jesus to heal.

This same God was able to set slaves free in Egypt and America as well as end segregation and create equal rights for minorities and women. Do we think God's power is now limited in today's time? Do we not think God, the Creator of heaven and Earth, of yesterday, today and tomorrow, can and will protect, redeem, and restore His children of every color and ethnicity? Revelation 5:9-10 reads:

> And they sang a new song, saying: "You are worthy to take the scroll, and to open its seals; for You were slain, and have redeemed us to God by Your blood out of every tribe and tongue and people and nation, and have made us kings and priests to our God; and we shall reign on the earth.

What painful offense do you need to personally lay down on the altar and give to God? God is a redeemer and restorer of every people group that is reconciled to Him. We need to ultimately trust God for our pains, injustices, and offenses rather than look to man to be the redeemer and restorer of people.

In his Dream speech, Martin Luther King, Jr said, "In the process of gaining our rightful place we must not be guilty of wrongful deeds. Let us not seek to satisfy our thirst for freedom by drinking from the cup of bitterness and hatred." Let God heal you of any offense, bitterness, and hatred that stems from the oppressions of life.

# CHAPTER 9

# COMPASSION

And Jesus, when He came out, saw a great multitude and was moved with compassion for them, because they were like sheep not having a shepherd. So He began to teach them many things.

MARK 6:34

Have you ever looked at a difficult situation and thought, *Someone has to do something about that*? If so, you have been moved by sympathy. Sympathy is a strong feeling of pity we experience when we see someone else's misfortune. But sympathy typically stops at a feeling and rarely translates into action. In the parable, it was compassion that compelled the Samaritan to help the wounded man, not sympathy. Reconciliation will never be accomplished through sympathy. Instead, we must learn to have true compassion for others. In the Bible, we do not read about Jesus feeling sympathy, but we repeatedly read about Him experiencing compassion. In the book *Live. Love. Lead.*, author and pastor Brian Houston writes the following about compassion:

Not one time do we ever find Jesus being moved with sympathy; but every time He was moved with compassion something powerful was about to happen—a miracle was on its way. That's because sympathy identifies with the problem, but compassion gets up, looks up, and says, "I need to do something about this."

## RECOGNIZE DISPARITY

There is a video that was created in November 2017 that went viral on social media. A group of diverse teenagers, including black, white, male and female, gather in what appears to be a youth learning activity. The adult leader lines the teens up for a race about 100 yards long, and the winner will get a one-hundred-dollar bill. The teens are excited to win the cash hanging in front of them. Every boy and girl of each race represented has a smile on their face at the starting line, with absolutely no division or animosity between them.

The adult announces that the winner at the finish line will receive the money, but he first would like to ask some prequalifying questions before yelling "go!" He asks the following questions, which allow each teen to take two steps forward or remain in place, depending on the answer: Were your parents married? Did you grow up with a father figure? Did you have a private education? Tutor? Did you fear your utilities being shut off? Did you have to help your parents pay bills? Was your ticket to college through athletics? Did you live life concerned about your next meal?

Through the line of questions, many teens happily take large leaps toward the finish line, getting closer to the reward. They do not notice the faces of those behind them, or the emotions of those only a few steps from the beginning or still waiting at the starting line. The leader takes a moment to ask those leading the pack several yards away to turn around. The students face each other with emotions ranging from guilt and sadness to anger and sympathy. The adult then states to the teens that the position they each have in this race has nothing to do with anything any one of them has done or decisions they have made up to this point in their lives. He tells them that it would be foolish for anyone in the front to believe they had not been given a better opportunity or head start to win this race called *life.*

He then makes a bold statement. He tells the students that every single one of them still has to *run their own race,* but some are given an advantage. As he is saying this, the viewer can't help but notice the disparity in color between the students standing at the starting line and those nearest the finish line. Several yards ahead of anyone stand mostly Caucasian males. In the middle, a mixture of females and males. The students standing still at the starting line, several yards behind everyone else, are overwhelmingly black males who initially believed they had a fair chance at the hundred dollars, just like everyone else. Tears of shame and frustration run down faces. Others allow pride to defend their anger.

The leader then tells them that this is a "picture of life." This is about the privileged versus the underprivileged, not black versus white, or any particular race. That said, it is difficult to ignore how significantly race impacted the results. Race is an ingredient in the imbalance in America today, impacting our starting point in life. Those of us who are privileged need to turn around and face reality, to see the disparity in life.

I was given the opportunity to perform these exact same exercises twice in my life: once in my late teens in college at a Campus Crusade camp in Los Angeles, California, and the second within corporate America at an office workshop, when I was married with a child on the way. The first time, I had no idea what the result would be. However, both times brought the same feelings of sadness, shame, and anger. Ironically, both times I was clearly the most distanced from everyone. In fact, in my exercises I was asked to take a step backward if the question did not apply to me. Both crowds consisted of white and black participants. I had additional questions asked, such as these: Can you buy your hair product in most local stores? Can the nearest salon fix your hair? Did your parents pay for your first car? I found myself, a biracial female, the farthest behind in the lineup of all people groups. My answers put me in last place, just like so many of the students in the video.

Granted, a white female friend from Colorado commented that her first car, gifted to her by her parents, was not brand-new but rather a beater. That can apply across the board on most of the questions. Not every married family has a perfect marriage. Not every father figure is a good example. Not every private school has quality teachers. The point overall, though, is the disparity of our starting point in life.

Where we start from has nothing to do with choice or behavior or attitude but rather the life circumstances that we are born into. Statistically, a higher percentage of blacks or people of color fall into this disparity in the U.S. That in itself cannot be ignored by those who are privileged, whether black, white, or yellow. Thankfully, my sons, who are of color and statistically considered black, are part of the privileged club. I say "thankfully" not to infer that privileged people are better than underprivileged people, but because I think most would agree it is better to have resources than not. My sons could answer yes to nearly every question on that video and that would put them at the front of the pack. In fact, they are more privileged than all the questions asked.

Being white does not mean you are privileged, nor does being black mean you are not privileged—that is, unless it is the color of your skin that created your opportunity or disadvantage. Unless it causes you to respond to someone differently. Unless a police officer chooses to pull you over because of the color of your skin. Unless someone chooses to say racist comments about you because of your color.

The point is, there are underprivileged people of every race, and those of us who are privileged have a duty to have compassion and grace for those who are not. They had no choice, played no role, and took no actions to put themselves in that position. Jesus said to whom much is given, much is required. We all have a responsibility to give grace and compassion to a brother or sister in need, regardless of race, but most especially to those who are being oppressed *because* of race. It was the Samaritan—the oppressed race—that chose to show compassion for his neighbor. He chose to use what he had been given to offer compassion and help to another.

## TAKE ACTION

Does giving grace or compassion mean giving money, a job, or a tax break? Maybe, maybe not. God knows. Does it mean taking my hard-earned money to give to someone who is lazy? Likely not. Proverbs 18:9 (NLT) says, "a lazy person is as bad as someone who destroys things." What about a sick widow, a veteran, or children being raised by lazy parents? Do we help them? It gets complicated. You may say, after all this, "Well, you overcame your circumstances of being underprivileged. Why can't others?" If you are truly asking out of curiosity, I will tell you. If not, it reveals a hard heart.

Here is my answer. I had an extremely encouraging father who told me my whole life that I could do anything I put my mind to. He encouraged me to be the best at everything. I am a firstborn with a firstborn mentality. My StrengthsFinder results say I am competitive. I have known Jesus since I was a child and I have prayed for wisdom since I was twelve years old. My dad also moved us away from crime-filled, low-income areas to protect us. What if my dad did not affirm me but harmed me? What if I was not comfortable fighting to get my way (middle children often are not)? What if I believed all the lies ever spoken about me and my circumstances? What if I didn't believe Jesus loved me? Or I lived in a community filled with crime, poverty, and high teen-pregnancy rates? Many youths with similar life circumstances had it much, much harder than I did—and without the support necessary to overcome an environment that can define you or, worse, destroy you.

How often do we take time to understand the factors of the environment others have had to overcome? Do we care? Are we compassionate and forgiving, or are we judgmental? What will it take for us to understand, give grace and compassion, and share wisdom despite any circumstance? Jesus is looking to you and to me. Jesus asked His disciples to pray for us, for you and me. They prayed for compassionate workers to harvest the fields.

> Then Jesus went about all the cities and villages, teaching in their synagogues, preaching the gospel of the kingdom, and healing every sickness and every disease among the people. But when He saw the multitudes, He was moved with compassion for them, because they were weary and scattered, like sheep having no shepherd. Then He said to His disciples, "The harvest truly is plentiful, but the labor-

ers are few. Therefore pray the Lord of the harvest to send out laborers into His harvest."

Matthew 9:35-38

There are harassed, sick, and helpless people who simply need someone to have compassion and lead them to the truth. There are some people who are making poor life decisions, and some born into those poor circumstances. The answer is in you and me. Compassion ignites us to action. Maybe it's time for you and me to stop looking around and start looking in the mirror.

As we saw with the good Samaritan, when we suffer, it gives us an opportunity to express compassion for others. If you are a person who has experienced suffering or discrimination, how much more generous should your heart be toward others who are also experiencing these things? A friend of mine, nearing sixty years of age, shared with me that she was the only African-American student in her childhood gifted program at an all-Caucasian school. There were several Jewish families as well. One day the class had a planned field trip to the neighborhood pool. A day before the trip the teacher apologized to her and told her she could not attend because she was black. Word got out and every single Jewish family withdrew their child from the field trip. In essence, they said, "Because we have experienced rejection too, we have compassion for you."

In the video I watched on social media, the leader tells the teens they still have to run their race in life. We all do. Some have a head start. Some do not. Once the leader finally says "go," those who started in last place take off running, using their *physical* gifts to overcome some of those who had a better start than they did. This is a picture of life. Many of us do not have a head start, but it does not mean we have to finish last. Between hard work and forming relationships along the way that help connect us to the right people and opportunities, we can also get ahead. Most importantly, there is no lack in Jesus when we submit our gifts to Him. Jesus Christ heals all wounds, financial lack, and health issues, but also racial oppression, financial oppression, and gender oppression. First John 2:6 says, "Those who say they live in God should live their lives as Jesus did." Jesus stormed the temple when the people were being taken advantage of.

Compassion stands for the one being preyed on due to race, age, disability, finances, or gender. Compassion is both humility and strength that allow you to forgive an offense and stand up for an injustice. Where do you need to provide compassion in your life? You are either part of the problem or part of the solution. What do you choose?

# CHAPTER 10

# RELATIONSHIPS

**Greater love has no one than this, than to lay down one's life for his friends.**

JOHN 15:13

Recently, my sister and I reflected on our entertaining panic-ridden attempt to invite neighbors to church for Easter one year. In our last-minute attempt to invite people to church, we realized there was no one in our circle of influence with whom we had a close-enough relationship to invite. Comically, it resulted in us desperately trying to decide how to ask the last waiter, cashier, or stranger at Walmart we saw on the way to church. We suddenly felt pressured and rushed to find *someone* in need of Jesus before Easter Sunday.

The truth is, we realized that we needed to be intentional to form relationships all year long, not in one day, one hour, or one moment. We needed to form genuine relationships and love people of all colors, all backgrounds, and all genders, not just to win them over but to actually care about them. Even if I had found some stranger to come to church that Sunday, then what? What if they joined the church? Then what? Would I genuinely be there to help them learn the faith, experience transformation, and become a disciple of Christ? Or would I just leave it up to my church and hope their programs, processes, and paperwork were in order to follow up and make sure the newly converted stranger did not fall through the crack? I am not against inviting strangers to church in any way; we just need to do a better job of genuinely caring about people long term.

Even the Samaritan in our parable demonstrated more than a momentary investment in his neighbor. He told the innkeeper that, upon his return, he would cover any additional expenses for caring for the wounded man. "When I return," he said. While we do not know the extent of his relationship with the wounded Jew after that moment, we do know that he intended to return and to ensure that the man's life was restored to him. In order to reconcile our nation and our hearts, we must be intentional about building relationships, understanding one another's experiences, being open and honest, and building bridges. This is what each of us needs to do in order to reconcile our churches and communities. Seek out unfamiliar relationships. Seek understanding. Be intentional. We heal through relationships.

## INTENTIONALITY

We have to be intentional in forming relationships. It is not easy to go out of our comfort zones and the circles we belong in. Sometimes we fall into the trap of imagining boundaries that we create ourselves. James and I were looking for a small group within our church when we first married and noticed there were some attended by more minority families and another that was attended mostly by white couples. I was tempted to join the small group with minorities because they looked like me; however, James reminded me that we needed to be intentional about forming relationships outside of the status quo. So we joined the group that did not look like us.

The discussions, relationships, and prayers that came out of that group of intentional and diverse individuals led to a depth of healing that went beyond race, status, or gender. The best friendships of my life were formed within that small group and helped shape the person I am today. We were intentional about forming relationships with people who were different from us, even if it did not feel natural initially.

Does everyone in your circle look like you, think like you, and have finances like you? Do you form relationships that are convenient and produced naturally in your environment? When was the last time you intentionally sought a friendship that was across the hall, out of your circle, or across the tracks? Sometimes we avoid relationships because of presupposition or judgments we carry about certain people or certain types of people. You may find yourself avoiding friendships with people you presume you do not like or with people who intimidate you. We all have experiences that lead us to develop beliefs about other people. Maybe because of your past you avoid friendships with police officers, pastors, residents of government housing, members of country clubs, Republicans, social activists. Who is that person for you? What do they look like? For me, I avoided friendships with wealthy, Caucasian *power women.* The more makeup, expensive clothing, and outward upgrades, the more intimidated I felt—especially if they were confident.

Being originally from Seattle, a more liberated, expressive culture, I was used to natural women who allowed their hair to actually gray, who didn't wear polish on their nails, and who wore neutral-colored clothing. Name brands and flashy clothing were not as important to my friends in high school. The cool thing to do was shop at thrift stores like Goodwill and Value Village. For fun we would look for the coolest throwback outfits we could find. My friends would creatively alter the rest. I remember one friend who ironed leaves on a slip to make a skirt. It was more important to try to be authentic than to run to the local Nordstrom and buy the most expensive item. That probably helped cover up my insecurity at not being able to afford Nordstrom.

When I moved back to Texas at age twenty-two, I had a preconceived image of women with big hair, orange polished nails, and makeup and wardrobes I could not pronounce. When it came to hair, makeup, and clothing in Seattle, I would compare it to an interpretative painting, the kind where paint is splashed and dashed everywhere—no rules, no regulations, but expressive; coloring outside the lines with freedom. In Dallas, it was more like coloring exactly inside the perfect lines, with precision. There were more rules, regulations, and standards.

I immediately judged women who looked perfect. I felt sure they did not like me, so I did not like them. If I could put up my fence first, then they could not make me feel less than. I was playing defense with my offense. Avoiding the desire to befriend these women hid my insecurity of feeling unworthy.

Until Judy came into my life. She was confident, wealthy, and wore the best wardrobes money could buy. She was a woman with great passion and dreams—a mover and a shaker. It was easy to judge her from a distance, to think she had no problems or that she did not have the time of day for anyone who did not live in her financial bracket. We had nothing in common (in my mind). I was younger. She was older. She was affluent. I was not. She was white. I was not. She had great influence in her community politically and socially. I was just a young girl with no clarity in my purpose, working in insurance.

What I did not know until I formed a relationship with her is that she and her husband built a business from the ground up. They spent their own hard-earned money building churches and orphanages each year around the globe. She spread the Gospel to women locally and in poverty-stricken nations. Most importantly, she loved like Jesus. She saw things in me I did not see in myself.

Once, she invited me to attend an intimate family trip where I was the only non-family member. I was confused as to why she would invite me. I was actually frustrated because it made me feel even more awkward and ashamed. I felt so different from the other women on the trip. I was sure that they were not my "tribe" of people. It amplified how I felt deep in my heart, although I pretended it didn't. I was tempted to feel like I was the token minority, there to meet a quota. I was proven wrong. To my amazement, I had an incredible experience and witnessed Judy's limitless gift of giving. She continued to invite me to her home, Bible studies, and even on vacations over the years. Though she never gave me a reason to believe she did not have my best interests at heart, I could not believe that she truly wanted to serve *me*. *Why me?* I would ask myself.

Here is why. Judy saw who I truly was. She saw the gifts and purpose on my life. She could see who I was when I could not see it for myself. She connected with my destiny and purpose, not the color of my skin, my age, or my background. Without even knowing it, Judy created a bridge. She was a natural bridge maker. She did it for countless women all over the globe in multiple cultures and nations. While I initially judged Judy and ran from her friendship, she saw me as God saw me and pursued me as God would pursue me. Over the years she has taken me under her wing, mentored me, and helped me see from a higher perspective: God's perspective. She was able to expose me to environments and atmospheres that connected me to my destiny, including writing this book, speaking, and teaching God's Word.

One of the greatest things Judy taught me was how to host and serve others in the home. She spares no expense to make others feel loved, comfortable, rested, and lifted up. At times, I have stayed at her home and cried because it was evident peace was there. It was the Holy Spirit. She had prepared her home just for that: for God's presence to dwell. The atmosphere she prepared left me feeling rested, restored, and encouraged. I am convinced that God purposefully sent me this friend, a woman who looked like the type of person that in the flesh—and maybe even historically—would have been an adversary. Instead, she was someone who would help me walk in healing and see myself the way God does, as a daughter of the King. She pushed me to seek God's voice, to serve others, and to move the Kingdom forward here on Earth. We now minister to women together.

Who or what type of person have you held yourself back from having a relationship with? Who do you need to pursue? God uses relationships to help us experience different aspects of His character. He also uses them to heal our wounds and insecurities. We cannot limit ourselves to relationships that make us feel comfortable. Encourage your children, friends, and family to be around people who do not look like them. Befriend people who are different from you and seek to understand their culture, traditions, religion, and what makes them special in God's eyes. This is not an attempt to convert them or you but for you to be educated and not ignorant. In my experience, when someone says something ignorant or discriminatory about another culture, it typically stems from their lack of knowledge or exposure, rather than hatred or racism. We often fear, judge, and even hate what we don't understand—or, simply stated, what we *mis*understand.

When living in Washington, I often heard stereotypes about Southerners. After we found out we were moving to Louisiana, friends told me I was going to live among nothing but swamps and snakes. I was terrified. When I lived in Texas, I heard locals refer to people from Asia as Orientals. I had to remind them that rugs are oriental, not people. Over nearly forty years, I have had the privilege of building friendships with people from a multitude of backgrounds and cultures: Korean, Vietnamese, Mexican, Puerto Rican, Panamanian, Belizean, black, white, mixed, Nigerian, Kenyan, Creole, and many others. This list is not as long or as wide as I would like it to be, but it is a start.

I want to create an atmosphere for my children to appreciate and love all cultures, even if they are not represented in our immediate community. My husband and I took our boys on a Caribbean cruise after our oldest graduated eighth grade. Both of my boys were blown away at the cultures they encountered. They played and ran around the cruise with youth from Ireland, Greece, the Caribbean, Jamaica, and other amazing places God created on this earth. The kids did not judge each other on their religion, politics, gender, or race. They just came into relationship with one another. It was their greatest takeaway from the trip. It sowed a seed I pray will continue to be watered for a lifetime.

## HONESTY

Relationships require honesty. As I mentioned previously, iron sharpens iron. That means that truth is embraced and received.

Proverbs 27:6 reads, "Faithful are the wounds of a friend, but the kisses of an enemy are deceitful." We have to live a life that allows our relationships to breed honesty. In order for communication to be authentic, we must allow others to speak truth into our life and situations. Reconciliation works the same way.

Denzel Washington starred in a film called *Remember the Titans*. It was based on a true story about a high school football team in Virginia that integrated a black school and a white school in 1971. My family and I recently had a chance to visit both the original building and the current high school a few miles away. Although much of the film is fictional, it captures the reality of the hostile time in our country during integration. While the end of segregation in schools was a victory for civil rights, the war was far from over.

In the movie, Denzel plays the role of the black coach who is moved districts to coach at the previously all-white school, T.C. Williams High. Coach Yoast, the white former head coach with a winning playoff record, is asked to assist Denzel as the assistant coach. The black players on the team see this as an opportunity to rise up and take leading positions they felt they had previously been denied. The white players coached by Yoast see this as a threat to losing their positions.

There is racism from both sides in the film, though many of the players attempt to reconcile throughout the movie. The leading characters who change everything are two defensive players: Julius is black; Gary is white. They are both seen as leaders by their teammates and within their racially divided groups. Initially, they both show prejudice and lack of tolerance toward each other. They argue. They fight. And they refuse to block or defend for the other race during practices or games. Denzel treats all of the players the same by disciplining them for the lack of unity. He requires players of the opposite race to room with each other and learn facts about each other's families to help unite them.

Julius and Gary do the bare minimum to get to know each other, just enough to avoid the punishment of running laps. However, something powerful happens at the climax of the hostility between the two boys. They are brutally honest with each other. Julius argues that Gary and his white friends are not blocking for Julius and his black teammates because they are black. Gary reprimands Julius, telling him that he is not working hard. While intense, the moment created an opportunity for both of them to be honest with each other, challenging each other to be better. After that conversation, Gary confronts his white teammates, telling them to block for the black players.

Gary gains Julius's respect as a real friend in that moment. He was willing to face his white friends with truth and honesty. Julius opens his heart to a white person maybe for the first time in his life. Their honesty opens the door to their relationship and eventually unifies the entire football team. They go on to have a winning season as an integrated football team. They set the example for the school to be unified during a racially tense time. Denzel tried to force the players to like each other. However, in order to form a real relationship, they had to create a place where they could be honest with each other and embrace the truth. Are you honest with yourself or embrace relationships that require honesty? When we form honest relationships, it will give permission to those we influence to do the same.

## BECOMING ALLIES

One very important piece of this puzzle is that Gary became an ally. He became an ally to his black teammates. Without his support and influence with the white football players, it is unlikely unity would have occurred on the team. Gary had to confront the evil that came out of the mouths and through the actions of his white teammates and his best friend, as well as his mother and girlfriend, who disapproved of his relationship with Julius. Many times, it takes an ally to stand up for the underprivileged in order for them to overcome.

Slavery did not end with just the support of the slaves. Harriet Tubman did not help slaves escape through the Underground Railroad on her own. Many of the safe houses were owned by white families who were allies in the fight against slavery. Women had men supporting them as they fought to gain the right to vote and other women's rights. Children require the protection and support of adults in order to be safeguarded from child slavery. Allies. Most wars are won when a nation joins forces with another, when they become allies against a common enemy.

Today, those who suffer injustice need an ally and an advocate. We all have an advocate in Jesus. And we also have one another. He sent you and me to be advocates through relationship. The unjust affairs and evil of this world can be conquered and overcome by a force of strong advocates and allies. Are you an ally who protects other people groups outside of your community, race, denomination, political party, gender, or financial status?

The Bible outlines the different covenant relationships we will experience during our lives. The first three will not surprise you, but the last one may: (1) God; (2) marriage; (3) children; and (4) brothers and sisters in Christ. If we realized that our family in Christ represents covenant relationships, we would likely treat them differently.

David Livingstone was a missionary in parts of Africa. All missionaries before his time were martyred in the region in which he chose to live. His solution was to make blood covenants with the local chieftains. He was the first to survive and live peacefully among the people, all because he made relationship a priority.

The traditional and historical process of making a covenant with another involved cutting the hand of each party and mixing blood. In biblical times, there were several steps in making a covenant. The first level of covenant was to give your cloak or coat to the other person, which symbolized provision and protection. Coats represented wealth and provision. The second level was to exchange belts, which typically carried weapons. This represented the laying down of one's weapon, but it also put both parties in a position of vulnerability. It said, *I won't hurt you and I cannot defend myself if you hurt me.* The last part of this covenant—that takes any relationship to the deepest level of intimacy—is the figure-eight walk. The two parties stood back to back, but as they walked in a figure eight to meet each other, they ended up face to face and eye to eye. This act was a vow to see each other, to communicate, to listen, and to seek to understand one another. Men would cut their hands to mix blood in a hand shake, sealing the covenant.

What a world of difference most marriages would be in today if we all promised to walk out such a covenant, not to mention relationships with friends and treaties with nations. Covenant communicates a very important message. It says, *I will be in relationship with you. I will protect you. I will not harm you. I will not retaliate. I trust you. I am your ally. I am your advocate. I will seek to understand. I will be intentional.*

In *Remember the Titans,* Gary's choice to become an ally to his black teammates opened the door to healing because it created a bridge. The bridge led to relationship, restoration, and reconciliation. It was a bridge of opportunity and possibility. It was a bridge of hope. However, even after all of the initiative, advocacy, and standing for what is right amidst his family and friends, reconciliation would not have been complete if Julius had not chosen to walk over the bridge created by Gary. If he had chosen to close the door, turn his back, or reject the hand extended to him, reconciliation would have been impossible.

This is how true reconciliation happens. First, someone has to create a bridge, then someone has to be willing to cross it. Reconciliation takes two. If your neighbor, whether black, white, Middle Eastern, police officer, or politician attempted to become your ally, would you cross that bridge, or would you turn down their extended hand and walk away? Has someone attempted to build a bridge that you have rejected? Has someone tried to reconcile, and you refused or ignored the attempts? Are you carrying anger, hurt, or unforgiveness that is holding you back from being free to walk across the bridge? It is time. God will guide you. It is time to accept allies to support, protect, and encourage you—because it is not just about your freedom but the legacy of freedom for the people who will follow.

We are meant to be reconcilers through relationship with one another. This is true in all areas of our lives. We are the hands and feet of Jesus. We have to accept the personal responsibility that we are God's plan in the earth to bring reconciliation through relationship. Let's extend an invitation of friendship to someone outside of our comfort zone and share our personal story. If we want to genuinely help someone, then we must genuinely seek to know them, love them, and serve them.

# CHAPTER 11

# THE RESPONSIBILITY OF THE CHURCH

Let there be no divisions in the church. Rather, be of one mind, united in thought and purpose.

1 CORINTHIANS 1:10 NLT

The Church is the bride of Christ and has a responsibility while here on Earth. We bring the greatest hope for all nations and people groups. The Church is the greatest resource of help and giving for a community, especially when disaster strikes. When churches are out of service, fall apart, or are ineffective and loveless, the community and people suffer and have no real hope. The Church must be united in reconciliation, standing for righteousness and pushing back darkness.

A divided Church cannot reconcile the world. Why would the world follow the Church if we are divided ourselves? We need reconciliation in the Church first before we can help our nation reconcile. We have to be united so we can stand tall as one, rise up, and fight the evil in this world. The world is counting on us to bring healing and set captives free as Luke 4:18 outlines. Jesus is the reconciler of racism, just like He is the redeemer of all transgression in our lives. He is the healer of all things. He is the ultimate reconciler and has given us the responsibility of reconciliation as well: "And he gave us this wonderful message of reconciliation" (2 Corinthians 5:19 NLT).

Jesus is a civil rights leader for women, children, rich, poor, local, and foreigner. We cannot be divided as a church racially or politically if we are to help the world fight its own demons. Jesus celebrates diversity so that we can use our diverse gifts to walk in unity, being interdependent upon each other to build His Church for Kingdom business.

In today's society, church and state are separate, which allows the government to rule on civil laws. However, the original moral code, from which most civil laws stem, is outlined in the Old Testament of the Bible. In biblical times, moral codes were upheld and judged by the priests, not the government. Their government was not separated from their faith. It was the people of God's responsibility to uphold all laws: moral and civil laws, as well as criminal or ceremonial laws. Jesus did not go to the governor but to the temple to proclaim truth. He went to God's house. He shared truth with the people of God. He challenged men and women of faith. He expected His house to respond. He encouraged His future bride to do His will. The Roman government did not even want to get involved with Jesus' ministry or persecution.

It is preferable that our government carries out the commands of God, and we should do our best to use our influence so that political leaders seek God; but we are held to a higher standard. It is the Church's responsibility to carry out the commands of Jesus Christ. It is not the responsibility of the government. We have allowed the

Church to be subject to the government, which rules and reigns over our land, rather than working in unity. King David would consult with the prophet to hear from God before going into battle or making important decisions. God was always meant to be our only King. He allowed an earthly king and government to be established only because His people asked to have a ruler like the nations that surrounded them (see Samuel 8). It was not God's plan, but God always gives us free will.

As a pastor, Martin Luther King, Jr. spoke to both the church and our government. That said, it was the government that responded and got involved in civil rights. Many churches and pastors stood with Dr. King, but many did not. Today, the most segregated place on a Sunday, around the nation, is in God's house. Look around at the churches in your community. How many of them are unified in representation of the different cultures of people that live in that same community? If your church is, congratulations! Most are not. Why does color or race matter in the Church when you share the same spiritual DNA? Could it be that the reason our nation is still so divided racially and politically is because it reflects the state of the Church?

Many of our churches have adopted the same offenses within political, social, and racial agendas as our nation and government. If your pastor cannot speak from the heart on racial and political issues from the pulpit without getting verbally attacked, something is amiss in the body. When our churches become breeding grounds for offense, it is time to make a change. When the government took it upon their shoulders to create justice during the Civil Rights movement, they only got so far. It was a short-term fix for a long-term issue. But maybe the Church was supposed to pick up where the government left off. The Church ultimately has to fight and destroy evil. We have the authority and dominion to do so, not the government. We have the love that conquers all. It is possible the Church allowed the government to place a bandage on a deep wound, and now that wound has turned into full-fledged disease. The weed was pulled off at the surface, but the root continued to grow until it now threatens to destroy our very *divided* United States of America. It is time for the Church to unite through the power of the Holy Spirit to bring true healing to the hostile racial, political, and social issues we face today. We carry the solution as the Bride of Christ. We must start acting like it.

The resurrected Christ addresses His bride in the second and third chapters of Revelation. Jesus loves us—the Church—so much that He revealed Himself in splendor and majesty to the disciple John so that he could write specifically to challenge and encourage us. In the book of Revelation, John identifies seven churches that deal with the following issues: lovelessness, persecution, death, works, lukewarm faith, compromise, corruption, and faithfulness.

Jesus tells the dead church that while they have a reputation for being active and alive on the outside, on the inside they are spiritually dead. He tells them to wake up, revive, and strengthen the remaining spiritual bones they have left. Both Jesus in the flesh and the resurrection tell us the same thing: faith without works is dead. He says to the dead church, "For I have found your deeds unfinished in the sight of my God" (Revelation 3:2 NIV).

This should hit home for many of us. This is not Paul or a disciple making a suggestion. These are the words of Jesus Christ, speaking to you and me. Works alone are not good enough, especially if we are spiritually dead. He goes on to suggest that those in the church will be at risk of missing His second coming: "Remember, therefore, what you have received and heard; hold it fast, and repent. But if you do not wake up, I will come like a thief, and you will not know at what time I will come to you" (Revelation 3:3 NIV). It would be a shame to work in the house of the Lord all your life and not truly be alive in Him. Let's wake up and do what Jesus has called us to do in His Church and in our nation.

## FIGHT FOR THE CHURCH

How can we fight for a fellow brother if we don't have enough courage to fight for our Christian faith? In current society, Christians are so used to being silent about what they truly believe, it is no wonder we are also silent on issues of injustice that are happening all over the world. I believe we need to remember that we are to be peacemakers and not just peacekeepers. Staying quiet is not the answer to unity. That is acquiescing, not making peace. If we are not careful, we will look like the compromising church Jesus spoke to in Revelation 2:12-17.

Jesus reprimands this church for compromising with the world's value and ungodly spiritual practices. His issue is that they allowed compromise, specifically, to enter into the church. If the Church loses its righteous standard, the world will have no real measure and the Church will lose its value. Jesus says in Revelation 2:16, "Repent, or else I will come to you quickly and will fight against them with the sword of My mouth." I do not think we want Jesus to fight against any of us. That is a terrifying thought. We cannot mix the world's beliefs together with God's. We have to show the world God's standards. Jesus tells this church that if they do, in fact, repent, He will give hidden manna and a new name and identity to the one who is victorious.

God will give us answers. Solutions. Provision. And He will re-name us. God will use our repentant hearts to do great things in the earth. The church that has compromised and become silent has the ability to repent and be a blessing once again. We cannot ignore what is going on around us though, especially the church, or we may find our own rights taken from us. In the Bible study *The Quest*, Beth Moore writes:

> In churches like mine, our privilege increasingly altered our perception and our perception increasingly altered our discipleship. Alteration was not intentionally misleading. It was the truth as many Christians in the prosperous West experienced it. Those (sacrificial and rigorous beginnings of church) were neither our experiences nor expectations. Meanwhile, Christians were being persecuted, tortured, and murdered in disturbing numbers on the same globe. We'd hear about them occasionally, and accordingly react with horror, but we struggled to see how our lives connected with theirs. We couldn't fathom such atrocities happening to us. However, here we sit, you and I, in a public atmosphere becoming increasingly hostile to the gospel. Some of those far away cruelties are not quite as comfortably far-fetched anymore. (p. 108)

It is easy to ignore what is going on across the globe, nation, or even across town when it does not directly affect you. However, without the church standing up for evil, it will spread. The old saying "If you don't use it, you lose it" describes the influence the Church may lose if we do not exercise our authority and responsibility to fight injustices locally and globally.

We also must stand and fight the persecution against the Church that will continue to increase as we draw nearer to the return of Jesus. The church in Smyrna—the persecuted church—dealt with great persecution from nonbelievers and the self-righteous. Jesus specifically says to them, "I know your afflictions and your poverty—yet you are rich! . . . Do not be afraid of what you are about to suffer. . . . Be faithful, even to the point of death, and I will give you life as your victor's crown" (Revelation 2:9-10 NIV).

The persecution, injustice, or pain here on Earth is only temporary, but He will reward us for eternity if we are faithful to Him! God calls us rich for our faithfulness to Him. Can you imagine standing in front of the King of kings as He says to you, "You are rich." There is nothing on this earth that could mean more than that. We do not prefer to suffer or go through persecution, but if we do go through it, how wonderful to know it was not self-inflicted or meaningless but had a Kingdom purpose.

My prayer is that pastors and leaders, around the globe and in our country, who have allowed their light to be extinguished under demonic pressures will have a spark of fire ignited in them to fight again. I pray that the true love of Jesus overwhelms them and that they have more fear of lost souls than of earthly persecution and compromise. Finally, I pray that they will not bow to dark influences convincing them to be quiet, that unconditional love will give them a fresh zeal to heal souls and our nation.

## RESPOND TO INJUSTICE

Speak up for those who cannot speak for themselves, for the rights of all who are destitute. Speak up and judge fairly; defend the rights of the poor and needy.

Proverbs 31:8-9

All four gospels of Matthew, Mark, Luke, and John tell us Jesus drove out money changers from the temple with a whip. Jesus became angry, but He did not sin. We refer to this as righteous anger. We should be upset and angry about sin and unjust issues in the world, resulting in us taking a stand against them. We cannot let our anger be focused toward each other but rather toward things that affect the Kingdom of God. At the temple, Jesus had a righteous indignation against the disrespect He encountered toward God, His temple, and ultimately the effect it had on worship. The money changers were taking advantage of the people's provision, lack of knowledge, and desire to please God. Jesus responded to the injustice He witnessed. As His bride, we must do the same: walk in meekness and strength, forgive a hurt, and defend the weak. We have to respond when someone is preyed upon because of their race, gender, or financial status. The Church cannot stay silent.

The very first church Jesus addresses in Revelation is the one not walking in love. Jesus tells this church that He does see all the good they do for Him. He sees all of the minute details down to the hard work, the patience, the endurance, the processes, the procedures, the challenges, the obstacles, the warfare. He acknowledges how proud He is of them for those things. He makes it clear, however, that what is even more important than all of the work the church accomplishes is their love for Christ and the people.

All of the work is in vain if we do not love. If we are caught up in the processes, battles, and warfare, and we forsake the love of the people and each other, then we are not pleasing Him. We are not doing His will. If we do not love the people in the church, how will we love the people outside of the church? Jesus makes a strong (and terrifying) promise. He will remove our influence, our light, and our impact if we do not love. We will be without purpose. Jesus holds the power to remove our influence if we do not carry out what we are called to do. Love responds to the needs of people. It is active and an attitude.

There are great heroes throughout history who became heroes because of their active response of love and righteous anger toward injustice. St. Patrick was one of those heroes. After falling victim to human trafficking in Ireland, he chose to do something about injustice. He responded out of love for people and opened 400 churches. He also took a stand against trafficking, which impacted the eventual abolition of slavery in Ireland. Another such example is Dietrich Bonhoeffer, a Christian who stood against the discrimination and killing of Jews in Nazi Germany.

Martin Luther is well known for his ninety-five theses that challenged the Roman Catholic Church in the sixteenth century, sparking the Protestant Reformation. Similar to Jesus' stand against the money changes, Luther objected to the selling of indulgences to dismiss sins, standing on the foundation that salvation was through faith and grace alone. He sought truth and chose to read the Word of God for himself. He did not allow anyone, including the Church, to corrupt God's Word and grace. It was not popular. It was not sanctioned. Eventually, Martin Luther was exiled for seeking the truth. Martin Luther King, Sr. chose to rename himself and his son, Martin Luther, Jr., after he visited Germany and understood the power of standing for moral justice and truth regardless of the world's approval. Later, his son also stood for truth. Dr. King was the greatest known leader in our country for moral truth, civil rights, and racial reconciliation.

All of these men lived lives that exemplified how the love of Christ—not hatred and offense—compels us to fight against injustice. The Church is the example to those observing the Christian faith and to those who are looking for answers. We have a responsibility individually as Christians and corporately as the Church. First John 3:18 (AMP), says, "Little children [believers, dear ones] let us not love [merely in theory] with word or with tongue [giving lip service to compassion] but in action and in truth, [in practice and in sincerity, because practical acts of love are more than words]." John is telling us it is not enough to use words that say we love others. We have to show acts of love ourselves, rather than waiting for someone else to do something. Merriam-Webster uses the following words to define the verb "do": carry out, execute, commit, exert, and produce. These are all active words, which means we cannot be passive. They are intentional. Responsive. Proactive.

Love rises up and does something. It does not respond out of fear. Doing something does not mean you have to get on an airplane or drive to another state where injustice is happening, though your convictions may lead you there. Taking action can look like making the phone call to your local politicians when injustices are being ignored by the government. It can look like donating money to help feed hungry children in Somalia where genocide is killing thousands; or providing Bibles for other cultures and languages; or donating backpacks filled with food for your local low-income school. Responding in love can look like a multitude of things.

When a prayer request comes across your phone, do you quickly pray to move on to the next text, or do you exert energy and drive to the hospital? When a teenager starts down the wrong path after losing a parent, are you willing to commit to spending time with them? When your neighbor experiences discrimination, are you willing to provide a listening ear? Doing nothing produces just that: nothing. We can do nothing, or we can decide to make an effort to really change the world one action at a time by doing something.

In order to do these things effectively for the Kingdom, we need to challenge ourselves as individuals and as a whole. The Church has a duty to examine its motives and effectiveness as the Bride of Christ.

Jesus told the persecuted church that they were rich. Interestingly, the lukewarm church refers to themselves as rich, just like the dead church professed to be alive. In the business world, there is a phrase for business owners who do well and no longer care to keep pushing to higher levels of success. We call them "fat and happy." This is what the lukewarm church was like. Jesus calls them blind, naked, poor, wretched, and miserable. He also tells them to repent. They act like they are wealthy, but only Jesus can make us rich. Jesus wants us to be zealous for Him and not allow our earthly treasures to make us content with our lives and be lukewarm. Those who are privileged—whether politically, financially, racially, or socially— are not excluded from the need to stand up and speak out against the unjust and the ungodly. A lukewarm church is not moving the Kingdom forward.

Churches need to speak in truth about today's issues and injustices, even if it is not popular or it causes us to be rejected or persecuted. But at the same time, *we* are the Church. You and I, individually and together—we are the Church. It is not only the lead pastor or elders who represent the Church. You and I are more representative of the Church than our pastors, because it is we who enter the rest of the world Monday through Saturday to share and display what we believe. We come to church on Sundays to receive the Word, inspiration, and teachings, but we are the ones who spread it to the world. This means we, as individuals, need to read the Bible ourselves. We need to seek God's truth. We need to know if what is taught on Sunday is accurate or not, because history has shown us that even the corporate Church has gone sideways at times, has

compromised with society, or has oppressed with a religious spirit. We have the power to discern God's truth, join together as the
Church, and respond to injustice. When it comes to responding to
and fighting injustice, we are more powerful together than as separate individuals. Let's unite as the faithful Church.

"Why have we fasted," they say, "and You have not seen?
Why have we afflicted our souls, and You take no notice?"
In fact, in the day of your fast you find pleasure, and exploit
all your laborers. Indeed you fast for strife and debate, and
to strike with the fist of wickedness. You will not fast as you
do this day, to make your voice heard on high.
Is it a fast that I have chosen, a day for a man to afflict
his soul? Is it to bow down his head like a bulrush, and to
spread out sackcloth and ashes? Would you call this a fast,
and an acceptable day to the LORD? Is this not the fast that
I have chosen: To loose the bonds of wickedness, to undo
the heavy burdens, to let the oppressed go free, and that
you break every yoke? Is it not to share your bread with the
hungry, and that you bring to your house the poor who are
cast out; when you see the naked, that you cover him, and
not hide yourself from your own flesh?
Then your light shall break forth like the morning, your
healing shall spring forth speedily, and your righteousness
shall go before you; the glory of the LORD shall be your rear
guard. Then you shall call, and the LORD will answer; you
shall cry, and He will say, "Here I am." If you take away the
yoke from your midst, the pointing of the finger, and speaking wickedness, if you extend your soul to the hungry and
satisfy the afflicted soul, then your light shall dawn in

the darkness, and your darkness shall be as the noonday. The LORD will guide you continually, and satisfy your soul in drought, and strengthen your bones; you shall be like a watered garden, and like a spring of water, whose waters do not fail. Those from among you shall build the old waste places; you shall raise up the foundations of many generations; and you shall be called the Repairer of the Breach, The Restorer of Streets to Dwell In.

Isaiah 58:3-12

In Revelation 2 and 3, Jesus began His letters to each church by pointing out what they were doing well, even though the rest of His letter brought discipline and correction. This should be an example of how we address people and the relationships in our lives. The second to last letter, written to the faithful church of Philadelphia, is extremely powerful and encouraging. Jesus quotes from the book of Isaiah and proclaims He is the one who opens and shuts doors. He commends the church for their faithfulness, despite those who speak against truth. He reminds them that He will deal with the evildoers and they will recognize His authority. Jesus promises to protect the church and then asks them to hold onto their faith, honoring them for their obedience. This letter is a complete contrast to letters written to the dead and lukewarm churches. This letter powerfully reflects how pleased Jesus is with His bride, the Church.

Like the faithful church in Revelation, we can be used as the vessels that lead His people to the gateway of eternity. Because of our role in bringing others to God, we need to remain steadfast, obey, and be faithful. I pray that God will help us all be a gateway to encountering Him, and not block it with being content, dead, or seeking to please the world. I pray that we will open doors God has opened and shut doors that God has shut. I believe God has opened a door for reconciliation and unity among His people so that His Church can continue to be faithful and do the will of God. In Matthew 24:14 Jesus tells His disciples that all nations will hear the Gospel, and then the end will come. We have the privilege to help Jesus' plan to return by reconciling the nations to Him.

It will take a united church to heal a divided nation. John 17 reveals Jesus' heart as He prays for our unity: "That they may be made perfect in one and that the world may know that You have sent Me and have loved them as You have loved Me" (v. 23). Jesus proclaims that unity through diversity will be the very evidence to the world that God exists. Only God could unite people who represent every culture, tongue, color, and class. When a large, diverse family works together as one, they become a witness to people who are also seeking unity and love. Most importantly, we must be united so that the world knows that God sent Jesus to be their eternal salvation and heal their wounds here on Earth.

# CHAPTER 12

# CHOOSING RECONCILIATION

**God blesses those who hunger and thirst for justice, for they will be satisfied.**

MATTHEW 5:6

During the 2017 NFL political and social feud of kneeling versus standing, a friend and I engaged in a very deep conversation at dinner. He is a Caucasian male and his father fought in the Air Force on top-secret missions and now likely has his name on foreign-enemy kill lists. What he shared with me is that he was very pained and angered by any NFL player who did not stand for the flag. To him, it felt dishonoring. His father had sacrificed his life for this country and the freedom they had to even play football (or, ironically, to dishonor the flag).

I did not take a position either way; I could feel my own opinions bubbling up. I decided to simply share the experience of the other side of the debate. I explained to him that the feelings were likely just as strong for the person who stands and the person who kneels. From my knowledge and experience, the man kneeling has a different experience of the American flag. That flag, in many cases, was built on the backs of their fathers. It was built on slavery, bondage, and racism. And the pain is only increased when discrimination of black men still occurs today.

As I shared this point of view, my friend stopped eating. He stared at me and said, "LT, I never thought of it that way. Wow. That is not my experience and I did not understand that perspective. I am so glad you shared that with me. That changes my perspective and I have empathy." We talked about it again later that week and he shared with me that our conversation truly was life-changing and eye-opening. I was extremely proud of him and had hope that more people can experience this reconciliation of viewpoints and perspectives.

My husband often reminds us that "it is better to understand than to be understood." I did not like the phrase early in our marriage because I was typically the one trying to make him understand. Now I embrace this philosophy not only in my marriage but also in friendships and business partnerships. I have achieved greater results, fulfillment, and success in all of these relationships by setting my agenda to the side, listening, and responding to the core issue at hand. It is a far more effective approach than defending, opposing, or pushing my own ideas. Listening is the key to hearing. Hearing allows you to genuinely and effectively respond to the real need in front of you.

I have started to participate in a dialogue process group called Living Room Conversations. It is teaching me how to hear. It allows participants to take time to become listeners and hear the experiences of those around us, truly engaging in their experiences. When we know someone's story, we have more compassion for their situation, history, and journey. It allows us to develop commonalities as people and to draw on a relationship rather than on preconceived notions. We have all had an opportunity to judge someone or their circumstance only to later hear their personal journey and correct our assumptions about who they are.

The group dialogue allows us an opportunity to lower the walls and barriers we've built in our hearts and minds and create a place of unity and compassion. I recommend this dialogue process group to small groups, churches, workplaces, and schools, all of which are places where discussions take place specifically around difficult and controversial topics. The group discussions are experience based. We choose not to focus on opinion or belief but on the experience of the people in front of us. Beliefs and opinions can be refuted and challenged. But no one can rob you of your experience in life. No one can drill a hole in your life experiences. They are real.

My husband and I are currently leading a youth discipleship where we lead the teens to draw out their opinions on certain topics. Then we ask them to share their experiences related to that same topic. This allows them the opportunity to share their reality. However, we then lead them to seek God's truth in the Bible on that topic. Opinions are not always truth. Experiences, while real, are not always God's best for us. His truth supersedes them all. We teach the youth that while we have certain negative life experiences, it does not mean that is what God wants for us in our lives. Sometimes we put ourselves in bad situations. It does not mean that is God's plan for our life. Other times our life story is compromised by the bad decisions of other people. That also is not God's best for our destiny.

While we all have life experiences that are real, we still have to align them with God's truth and what He says for our lives. In her book *Unashamed*, Christine Caine clarifies it in this way:

Hurt people hurt people. Broken people break people. Shattered people shatter people. Damaged people damage people. Wounded people wound people. Bound people bind people. Offended people offend people.

Found people find people. Healed people heal people. Helped people help people. Rebuilt people build people. Whole people restore people. Loved people love people. Freed people lead others to freedom.

Which one are you? Which one will you become? A young girl who was abused growing up may walk into a life of prostitution. While hearing her life story would bring compassion—instead of judgment—to her situation, we would want to help her move into God's truth for her life. We would want her to know that He set her free of all oppression. A young boy may have witnessed a life of drugs, gangs, and violence, leading him to a life spent in and out of prison. Again, when listening to his heartbreaking story, it should lead us to compassion for him and the broken life he endured. But it doesn't end there. We would want to help him walk in forgiveness and restoration, God's higher purpose for his life. His story may also lead us to help young boys in that same type of community so that they do not fall prey to the same traps but instead break free to have a better chance at living out God's plan for their lives. We need to hear people's stories for connection and compassion and to unify them to the Truth. Opinions alone are worthless. Experiences are just the beginning. Seeking God's truth—and doing something about it—is the answer.

While I was writing this book, my son shared with me that he did not like being one of the only boys of color in his school. It was a great opportunity for me and my husband to evaluate. Were we doing our jobs as parents to educate him on handling racial comments? Did we put him in an environment that celebrated diversity? Did we take the time to help him see God's perspective in all of this?

This is not just a book. This is real life. I had to dig deep into my soul as a mama to ask God for His perspective as well. So many thoughts ran through my mind. Should I approach the parents of the kids who speak in ignorance? Do we need to move him to another school? Do we need to move to another city that is more diverse? Where God led me was to remember how James and I had pushed through similar issues years ago when it came to relationships.

Relationships are purpose-driven, not race, age, or gender-driven. If the spirit has connected, then the flesh does not matter. Only the flesh tries to restrict, define, and limit relationships according to our differences. The spirit connects our hearts, our purpose, and our destinies. Therefore, relationships in our lives will reflect diversity if we are led by God. We need people who are different from us to help us accomplish what God has created us for. We need others to strengthen our weaknesses and sharpen our iron.

The easy answer would be for me to put my son in an environment where others look like him, think like him, and have the exact same experiences as him. We typically desire to be with others who can identify with us and understand our struggles. Putting my son around other minorities might help him feel understood. Maybe they could relate to that awkward moment in class when he was learning about slavery and the teacher and students slowly turned and stared at him—the only black kid in the class. Instead, what if we taught our children, family, friends, and community to walk in compassion and seek understanding like Jesus did? We would not need everyone in our circle to look or talk just like we do.

For years, many of my closest friends attended the same church. Over the years, however, several have transitioned to other churches. The question I faced was whether we could or would continue to be in relationship despite our differences. I choose to love and partner with my sisters in Christ no matter their church, denomination, race, or political party. Today, my best friends, who offer me counsel, wisdom, and direction, do not attend my church, share my political opinions, or have the same color skin as I do. I do not seek out their similarities in the flesh but in the spirit. When I need to hear a word from the Lord on a life-altering decision, I need to stand with a friend who hears from God. That has no bearing on race, politics, or socioeconomic status. This is the lesson I continue to teach my sons. It is the message of Jesus Christ.

In the worst performing year of my profession, I dug the deepest, learned the most, and built the most rewarding relationships than when I was in my prime years, exceeding my goals by large margins. My performance goals in this particularly difficult year were unrealistic, even from the very beginning of the year. I could have chosen to give up—which was a real temptation—because the feeling of defeat was so great. But I didn't. I pushed through and came out stronger. Sometimes it is in the hardest, most divided, most difficult times in our lives that we find solutions, relationships, and character that we might not have otherwise encountered. We have that opportunity now. Our challenge is to dig deep to uncover the buried treasure of reconciliation within ourselves, churches, community, and nation.

## BECOMING THE GOOD SAMARITAN

The definition of a good Samaritan isn't someone who is inherently good, but someone who chooses not to be offended. It is someone who, despite prejudice and persecution, chooses to overcome and not return the same behavior. It is a choice to live a certain way, despite that person's encounter with the good, bad, and ugly of humankind.

Now what if the beaten-down, discriminated, prejudiced, wrongly accused, generationally oppressed, and rejected *half breed* walked in offense? What if deep in his soul he was offended from all the hurt, pain, and abuse from the white race, privileged race, ignorant race, or selfish race? How would he have responded differently? Would he be justified? Would he change the world or continue the same trap set for him as his offended forefathers?

If you have been rejected, hurt, or fallen victim to discrimination, racism, or prejudice, there is good news. Jesus is our good Samaritan. He was spat on, beaten, mocked, offended, completely rejected, and murdered. He knows exactly how you feel. He knows your pain. He knows your afflictions. He knows your discrimination and injustice. He chose to give His life to heal our wounds and our afflictions when no one else would. He did it for you, me, and even for those who continue to reject Him. Brothers and sisters, the good news is shared in Luke 4:18, where Jesus boldly declares the prophecy of Isaiah 61:1. He came to set the captives free!

> The Spirit of the LORD GOD is upon Me, because the LORD has anointed Me to preach good tidings to the poor; He has sent Me to heal the brokenhearted, to proclaim liberty to the captives, and the opening of the prison to those who are bound.
>
> Isaiah 61:1

You and I are free in Jesus Christ! There is freedom for our children and freedom from the generational curses bestowed on any of our families. In Isaiah 61, the prophecy continues, and we learn that God desires to restore what has been taken from you.

> To proclaim the acceptable year of the LORD, and the day of vengeance of our God; to comfort all who mourn, to console those who mourn in Zion, to give them beauty for ashes, the oil of joy for mourning, the garment of praise for the spirit of heaviness; that they may be called trees of righteousness, the planting of the LORD, that He may be glorified. And they shall rebuild the old ruins, they shall raise up the former desolations, and they shall repair the ruined cities, the desolations of many generations. . . . Instead of your shame you shall have double honor, and instead of confusion they shall rejoice in their portion. Therefore in their land they shall possess double; everlasting joy shall be theirs.
>
> Isaiah 61:2-4, 7

Who do you choose to place your hope in for all your needs? God will redeem every tear, every pain, every rejection, every insult, every offense, every unjust thing—if not here on Earth, then when we get to heaven. He will turn our mourning into joy and provide beauty for the ashes heaped upon us while here on Earth. No matter what anyone has done to you or your family, you will receive blessings and joy from your Lord and Savior Jesus Christ if you give it to Him. The praying people during slavery, both slave and abolitionist, prayed to God to end slavery. Many did not get to see slavery abolished personally, but their children and grandchildren did. Your legacy will see the fruit of your prayers.

Psalm 27:1 says, "The LORD is my light and my salvation; whom shall I fear? The LORD is the strength of my life; of whom shall I be afraid?" Despite our enemy's attempts to divide us, break us, and oppress us, Jesus has set each of us free and given us the ability—through His love, authority, and power—to unite and bring healing to each other. We cannot be healed if we allow offense to steal our hope in the Lord.

We can all identify with the Samaritan—the half breed—because we all live in the same divided and fallen world. It is not about race or ethnicity, history, or economy. We can all identify with lines of division that we have created in our own minds or that others have placed on us. I imagine you have placed one foot on both sides of the spectrum at some point in your life. We are all "mixed" in our own way. Did the thought ever cross your mind that Jesus was the most drastically mixed person of all? All God. All Man. All heavenly. All earthly. That gives Him the authority to heal all the divides that could ever try to separate us from each other, from our purpose, or from Him.

He is the half breed who identifies with brokenness and has compassion to heal the world. We all have hurts, wounds, and regrets that have led us to be cast out, rejected, or divided. It is from this place of pain and division that we can open our hearts to walk with Jesus to a place of healing and in unity. It is out of brokenness that we can provide wholeness.

Love compels us to fight against injustice, love our neighbor, reconcile the nations. It is our responsibility. It is time for us to examine our hearts, let go of offense, and offer forgiveness to our broken and divided world.

For the sake of our families, community, and nation, we must become the good Samaritan to those around us. Will you join me?

# NEXT STEPS

As you finish this book, you may be asking yourself, *What's next? What do's do I do? Where do I start? What needs to be done? What can I do?* First, I congratulate you for the desire to walk in love and do something. It takes just one person, one step, one moment, one day, one life at a time. You will influence and impact others, who will then impact one life, one day at a time as well. Before long, we will be the light like a city on a hill, leading our nation.

I have created a simplified to-do list to help you and others on this journey. Consider walking through it with a small group, with your family, or with your neighborhood with the intent to walk in love in perfect harmony (see Colossians 3:14).

To do:

1. Accept the personal responsibility as Jesus' ambassador in this earth. You are the good Samaritan here on Earth. Be a reconciler. Help others find reconciliation.

2. Share your personal story. Encourage others to share their stories. Show compassion and seek truth. Educate others on real-life experiences. Listen to real-life experiences.

3. Develop an intentional relationship with people you typically ignore or even those toward whom you have contempt, prejudice, or racist thoughts and feelings. Listen. Hear. Repent.

4. Do something that will bring healing, reconciliation, and unity for God's Kingdom. Don't be a passive peacekeeper but rather an active peacemaker. Respond out of love.

5. Read the Bible to find truth for yourself. Do not depend on opinions or assumptions, whether your own or from others. Do not react to social media or the negative news.

6. Host or join a Living Room Conversation dialogue. Visit *Livingroomconversations.org* to learn how to respect, relate, and connect across divides.

7. Be an ally. Create bridges and fight for justice for other people.

At the end of each letter written to the seven churches in Revelation, Jesus says, "Whoever has ears, let them hear what the Spirit says to the churches." What do you hear the Spirit saying to you, His bride, the Church? Jesus gives the same advice in Matthew 7:24: "Therefore whoever hears these sayings of Mine, and does them, I will liken him to a wise man who built his house on the rock." You have heard the word of Jesus—what will you do now?

# AUTHOR'S NOTE

Be obedient and write visions, dreams, and messages that God gives to you. You never know when you will use them. Much of this book was written with me simply reading journals for the past two years, recalling these events or what God put on my heart at that time. I had no idea why or if I would ever share it; and now I am sharing it with the whole world. God's Word is not just for you: you are a vehicle to His plan. What a glorious honor it is to be used by Him to bring His healing and reconciliation to the earth He created. I finished my first draft of this book on MLK Day. Coincidence? I think not.